Learning Curves

Learning Curves

Living Your Life in Full and with Style

Learning Curves

Living Your Life in Full and with Style

MICHELE WESTON

WITH MICHAEL SHELDON

CROWN PUBLISHERS
NEW YORK

Grateful acknowledgment is made to the following for permission to reprint previously published material:

Frances Berg: excerpt from "Nondiet Movement Gains Strength" by Frances Berg, *Healthy Weight Journal*, September/October 1992, 6:85–90. Reprinted by permission of the author.

Laura Fraser: excerpt from *Losing It: False Hopes and Fat Profits in the Diet Industry* by Laura Fraser. (New York: Dutton, 1997.) Reprinted by permission of the author.

Camryn Manheim: excerpts from *Wake Up, I'm Fat!* by Camryn Manheim. Copyright © 1999 by Camryn Manheim. (New York: Broadway Books, 1999.) Reprinted by permission of the author.

Random House, Inc.: "Phenomenal Woman" from *And Still I Rise* by Maya Angelou. Copyright © 1978 by Maya Angelou. Reprinted by permission of Random House, Inc.

Published by Crown Publishers, 201 East 50th Street, New York, New York 10022.
Member of the Crown Publishing Group.
Random House, Inc. New York, Toronto, London, Sydney, Auckland
www.randomhouse.com
CROWN is a trademark and the Crown colophon is a registered trademark of Random House, Inc.

Printed in the United States of America

Design by Elizabeth Van Itallie / Hello Studio

Library of Congress Cataloging-in-Publication Data
Weston, Michele.
    Learning curves : living your life in full and with style / by Michele Weston with
Michael Sheldon — 1st ed.
      1. Body image.   2. Overweight women—Psychology.   3. Obesity—Psychological aspects.
    4. Feminine beauty (Aesthetics)   5. Self-esteem in women.   I. Sheldon, Michael.   II. Title.
    BF697.5.B63 W47   2000
    646.7′0082—dc21

                                               99-046061

ISBN 0-609-60580-1

10 9 8 7 6 5 4 3 2 1

First Edition

To my parents, family, and friends, for their love and support, for honoring my struggle to become who I am and to live life with my own style. To my Papa Harry, for passing along the gift of knowing that a picture's soul lies in the subject's eyes.

Also, to the millions of women around the world who are all on learning curves. May you find your path and your style and be the women you are truly meant to be.

Special Acknowledgment

One of the greatest discoveries I have made during this part of my learning curve has been with my writing partner, Michael Sheldon. He was my guide, teacher, and friend, in being able to truly see me, hear me, and honor the experience with such grace and dedication. Michael, you made order out of chaos, and I thank you for putting this book's profound message on paper with me. To Derek Anderson, my business partner, in helping me realize my vision, in holding the boat steady and guiding me through the rough channels, for reminding me that I had already traveled so far and that I could make a difference with my experience, words, and voice. To you both, for holding me through the darkness, and for knowing that there was always light at the end of the tunnel. You helped me to go back to the center, breathe, and feel the power of self-love. For everything, I am eternally grateful.

Acknowledgments

(in no special order)

With thanks to Allison Anders, Kim Coles, Camryn Manheim, Molly O'Neill, Yvette Freeman, Delta Burke, Kathy Najimy, and Emme, whose stories and support acted as my guiding light throughout the writing of this book.

To Dee Dee Knoche, Barbara Brickner, Kate Dillon, Susan Moses, Angellika Morton, Wendy Shanker, Vanessa Marshall, Audrey Smaltz, Anna Scholz, Nikki Bordeaux, Wickham Boyle, and Marie St. Victor, whose courage and strength have been an inspiration.

Thanks to Nelson Mandela, Marianne Williamson, and Maya Angelou for their prayers. They have encouraged me to uncover my purpose and reveal my gifts.

To Patricia Albere, my spiritual teacher, and all the people with whom I have spent the last five years, for showing me how strong my connection is to Spirit. You have all shaped the course of my journey.

Profound thanks to Bruno Gaget, Jacqueline Caddick, Joe Iannitti, Donna Simchowitz, Liis Windischmann, Kaete Montgomery, Maiysha Simpson, Patrick, Jacqueline, Robert, and Eric, for helping to create the most beautiful pictures, and to David Pfendler for the wonderful illustrations.

My gratitude to my agent, Susan Golomb, and my editor, Ayesha Pande, first for "getting it," and also for their invaluable insights into the world of book publishing. To Tina Constable and her team, and to Sandi Mendelson, for putting me out there even further to deliver my message.

Thanks to Nancy LeWinter and Julie Lewit for allowing me to play such an integral part in the magazine-publishing revolution that became *Mode*.

A special thank you to Sylvia Heisel, Brian Bailey, Richard Metzger, Russell Kemp, Brenda Kett, and Michael Akers for their new vision in fashion design.

Thanks also to Gary Dakin, Susan Georget, Jeffrey Weinberger, Angie O'Reilly, Judy Molnar, Bobbie Hill, Casey Maher, Catherine Lippincott, Richard

Kestenbaum, Vincent Kirsch, Julie Priddle, Susan York, Nancy Lublin, Liria Mersini, Jim Roi, Evyan Metzner, Maryellen Gordon, Lori Goldstein, Neil Flaum, Julianne Fenhagen, Joyce Luft, Ted Gibson, Tracy Reese, and my mentor, the late David Karsten.

I can't even begin to list all the men and women who have touched my life, made me strong, helped me, shown me the way, and inspired me to share my story. To them: You hold a special place in my heart.

Contents

Our worst fear is not that we are inadequate. Our deepest fear is that we are powerful beyond measure. It is our light, not our darkness, that most frightens us. We ask ourselves, "Who am I to be brilliant, gorgeous, talented, and fabulous?" Actually, who are you not to be? You are a child of God; your playing small doesn't serve the world. There is nothing enlightened about shrinking so that other people won't feel insecure around you. We were born to make manifest the glory of God within us. It is not just in some of us, it is in everyone, and as we let our own light shine, we unconsciously give other people permission to do the same. As we are liberated from our own fear, our presence automatically liberates others.

MARIANNE WILLIAMSON
READ BY NELSON MANDELA IN HIS
INAUGURATION ADDRESS, MAY 10, 1994

THE LENS THROUGH which I view my body and my life has changed forever. For the last fifteen years, I have been on a journey—the journey to find happiness with and within my bigger body. I traveled far and wide without leaving New York City. The places I visited didn't require a passport or a suitcase full of clothes. All I had with me was a mirror, my memories, and a journal. They would unravel the secret that I had for so long wanted to reveal. The search was to find my beauty and my style. What I found in the process was all this and much more.

My discoveries have culminated in *Learning Curves.* This book documents each step I took in order to find fulfillment in the fuller figure I am now proud to own. Like most journeys, there were days of sunshine and days of rain. There were moments when I wanted to go back home, cut the journey short, and begin again at a later date. But I didn't. Because I knew that if I chose not to complete the journey, my life would continue to be marred with unhappiness and insecurity. Creating a life that would make me truly happy required letting go of the negative beliefs that had caused me pain. It was this desire that kept me searching.

I have met thousands of plus-size women in the last three years through working at *Mode* magazine. Whether I've been commentating fashion shows across the country or at the office finding clothes for the magazine to cover, all of them inspired me to continue my journey to feel beautiful inside and out. This book is a product of their encouragement, support, and love. The experience of writing *Learning Curves* now gives me the opportunity to inspire every full-figured woman to find her true style.

Twenty-two of the women whom I have encountered over the last ten years inspired and guided me in my journey to find self-love, self-style, and self-assurance. I know their stories will do the same for you. Some of these women are friends I have come to know well, and others are women I have met only briefly. But all have touched my life deeply.

Each of them took a different leg of the journey with me because each had a unique and profound experience of the particular subject at hand. Whether one woman was learning how the past was still creating her current reality or another had learned how to be comfortable with her body, each of them reveals how she found freedom and her own style from the lessons her experiences taught her. Their stories punctuate the eight steps of this book's learning curves. These women are all big, all beautiful; some are famous, some not; they cross the divisions of age, race, and occupation. But all are extraordinary in their capacity to celebrate who they are and embrace living fully and feeling beautiful in their bodies.

The eight steps that have enabled me to find my beauty and style encompass the learning curves that I invite you to take. I will be your guide, and will take you by the hand and show you every step of the way. As a big girl myself, I know what it's like to have the world slap you in the face because of your size. I have suffered the pain of being told that I couldn't fit in because of my weight and I have felt the frustration of believing that the only way I could be measured was by a number on the bathroom scale. I bought into that beauty myth. I have lived with the shadows of my own past, weighed myself morning and night, dieted and binged, been over-looked at dances, and have been ignored at times by a world that has seen beauty only on a very small scale. But not anymore. These eight steps have given me the power and the permission to feel beautiful. I wouldn't change myself for the world.

Here are the eight steps, included in which are twenty-nine learning curves. Each will bring you closer to feeling and looking beautiful. Step 1 asks you to understand how your past has shaped how you see yourself today. You can only look forward to a life of feeling beautiful once you've looked back at where your fears have come from. Step 2 invites you to create the life you've always dreamed about, free from the limitations that many full-figured women face. It shows you how to begin living your life through your own lens and guides you through the search to find your inner style. Step 3 looks at your body. You will see that by learning to embrace the parts you love and accept the parts you don't, you will have taken an incredibly important step toward finding self-love. You will learn how to own your body on *your* terms. These first three steps test your courage, self-worth, and capacity to feel beautiful. I assure you that the journey is well worth completing, because you will then begin to realize how to feel beautiful, how to make your life rich and fulfilling, and how to love your body.

Step 4 looks at your attitudes with regard to food, exercise, and the way your body vocabulary expresses how you feel about yourself. You will be shown how your feelings about each of these subjects hold the key to unlocking a life of health, enjoyment, and celebration free from guilt.

Steps 5 and 6 reveals your style through dress. You will take a tour of your wardrobe, uncover your personal taste, and I will show you how clothes can make you look and feel your most beautiful.

Step 7 looks at how you can date with style. By exploring the attitude of feeling desirable, the clothes you wear on a date and the date itself will show you how to radiate style and how to attract the attention of another.

Step 8 invites you to see yourself in relation to those around you. This final step asks you to view yourself as a role model. You will see the woman you are and appreciate that your beauty is seen not just by you but also by those who love you.

Having completed the learning curves journey, I have returned to a place where I can bask in the light of my own radiance. It is as brilliant as the dawn of the new millennium itself. I can tell you that I feel beautiful, powerful, purposeful, and original. I now am able to live my life out loud, in full, and with style. My hope is that you will feel the same way about yourself as I now feel about myself. If I can help one woman to feel her power and beauty and see herself in a new light, I will know that this book has made a difference and that my purpose in writing it has been achieved. I hope that woman is you. By reading this far, you have already started your journey. Learning your curves with me urges you to see life in a different light—*your* light, *your* truth. This is *your* life. So live it in full and with style.

Step 1

Learning from Your Past

I don't think you can possibly come to terms with the body you have or even have the body you really desire, for very long, if you don't go back and look at your past. Feel all the places where you weren't accepting of yourself and others weren't accepting of you. Go back and feel the pain that was in your body. Discover and discard those old ideas. See where you came from. Only then can you heal yourself and forgive others. Learn to live in today and not in "later on."

ALLISON ANDERS, FILM DIRECTOR AND SCREENWRITER

PAST EXPERIENCES CONTROL YOUR PRESENT REALITY

If you really want to start living your life in full today, the journey always begins by looking in the back of your "closet." By that, I mean identifying and then exorcising the ghosts and shadows of your former self. As you take this journey with me, I ask only two small things of you. The first is to make a commitment to read one section (no, not one whole chapter!) of this book each day, be it on the bus, on the plane, before bed, or after breakfast. You choose. The second is that you complete the exercises contained in each section. That's all.

My desire is both to inspire you to look at yourself, your body, your worth, and your life and to reveal to you the beautiful woman who lives within you. She who has always lived within you. The techniques I will use, step by step, exercise by exercise, will uncover the woman who has been masked. I have learned these techniques with the help of experts, therapists, healers, my spiritual teacher, and my network of full-figured women. The exercises have transformed my own life into one full of joy, purpose, and style. I will show you how you can change yours.

Take this book with you, wherever you are, wherever you go, and be sure that these pages become part of your reference. Use this book like a travel guide. After all, this is your journey. Look for new roads and avenues, a new language and different styles of expression. Take the opportunity to explore another path—one that you haven't yet traveled down.

In order to untangle the web that ties your past to the present, you have to look back. Psychologist and author of *Transforming Body Image: Learning to Love the Body You Have* (Trumansburg, NY: Crossing, 1995), Marcia Germaine Hutchinson, whose workshops I have attended, says, "You have to peel away the obstacles to seeing your body as an acceptable, comfortable home." Your current life is an amalgamation of everything that's happened in the past. Every thought, opinion, doubt, and fear can be traced back to a single moment, a singular act, and those times in your life have shaped the way you see yourself today. You may still believe that you're untidy because you never cleaned your room, or that you're clumsy because you once tripped on a stair.

For years, I felt fat and unworthy. I could trace those beliefs back to the time when I was thirteen and I went into my mother's closet, looking for an outfit to wear for a family dinner. I found a pair of pants that I had always loved to wear, only to feel devastated by the fact that they no longer fit me. Even though the pants were a size ten, I felt I had gone into the never-never land of double digits. That meant heartache because I would never be like the other girls who wore a size five or seven. I would go to stores with my friends, thinking I didn't deserve new clothes. Through early adulthood, no matter what the number on the tag in my clothes read or how beautifully dressed I was, all I could see was me, the fat girl, bursting out of my mother's pants. My vision was colored by the filter of the past. Only when I chose to go back and remember that painful memory could I begin to realize that I was no longer that little girl. Releasing that memory freed me from that negative experience and allowed me to see who I am today.

If you're brave enough to bring some of your unpleasant memories into the light of day, you, too, will be able to see them for what they are: things that happened in the past. Your reward for looking back inside your closet will be a life not determined by the past, but created by you today—the fulfilling, rich, and happy life that you want and deserve. I'd like to share some stories from the women I have met. These stories demonstrate the power of a past experience and the impact it still has on them today.

Dee Dee Knoche is the redhead who got on a bus in Texas and came to New York at seventeen years old, determined to make it as a makeup artist and model. She is a woman who, at her wedding, announced of her hairdo, "The higher the hair, the closer to God!" She is as sweet and light as cotton candy and has taught me that life is like an amusement park. The other rides aren't nearly as scary once you've experienced the one that turns your heart upside down.

DEE DEE'S STORY

An experience of a day with my father has been the sole cause of all my problems in relation to love. A woman's first relationship with a man is with her father. I was thirteen. My parents had been divorced for ten years and I visited him in a suburb in Texas for the weekend. He drove his Corvette up the driveway and said that we were going for a ride. I was thrilled at the thought of finally spending some time alone with him. He said nothing to me in the car as we drove away. He seemed angry as we pulled up to his office. My daddy is a chiropractor. We went in; he turned on the lights and pointed to the scale. "Get on!" he yelled. I was mortified. As the scale rolled over to read 185 pounds, I looked at him, humiliated. His voice boomed, "You weigh as much as a man! You'll never get a man! No man's going to love you!" Including him.

Afterward, he took me home. I felt traumatized. He locked me in a room for the rest of the afternoon and started playing subliminal weight-loss tapes. I cried and cried. He stood there watching. My stepsister peered through the window and laughed as I wept. It was the ultimate in cruelty. Years later, I started dating Ramsey. I suspected early on that he'd be the man I would marry. I was happy and gained thirty pounds. I thought for sure he would be appalled and disgusted and dump me. In that moment, I realized that I was still reliving that day with my father. That I was defective, a nonperson, and completely worthless if I was fat. It was remembering what had happened that one weekend that made me realize how destructive a past experience was in creating my current reality.

Sometimes our past is so painful that living in the present is a daily ordeal. Though some experiences can be switched on or off in our minds, others run like a long reel of film. Take Allison Anders, for example. I met her just as she had finished a movie. She wrote the screenplay for *Grace of My Heart,* and directed it. This movie is about a woman exploring her identity through writing songs. We were introduced to each other by a mutual friend. Allison was quiet, intense, and someone who was ready and willing to walk me through the pain of her past. She has raised a family single-handedly, adopting a young boy whose mother had died of AIDS after one of Allison's previous films. I continue to be motivated by the passion she feels for her craft. Her life experiences not only act as inspiration for her work but also provide a vehicle for her to work through her issues and overcome the obstacles in her life.

ALLISON'S STORY

This isn't easy for me to say. At twelve years old, I was raped. Raped by two brothers who lived in my hometown. They grabbed my shoulders from behind and pinned me down. Such trauma has left me deeply shattered. Ashamed of my body, nervous in my mind, separate from the people who love and support me.

Several years ago, I was working on a movie. I sat in my director's chair, and just as we were to begin filming, a crew member came up from behind me and grabbed my shoulders. I jolted and screamed at him. In that moment, I realized I was reliving the rape scene. My current reality is still connected to that day in the hallway of those kids' house, the day I was raped. Whenever I begin directing a new movie, I gather the cast and crew (which isn't easy when you've got Madonna standing in front of you) and tell them that there is something they need to know before we begin. No one, and I mean *no one,* is to come up behind me and touch my shoulders.

Even if it's a spontaneous massage. I don't like being caught by surprise. I don't tell them why. They always respect my plea. Every time someone takes me by surprise, I find myself back at age twelve, defenseless and traumatized.

Barbara Brickner is the model whose relationship with her mother most loudly echoes my own relationship with mine. We grew up in different parts of the country—she in Washington State riding horses and I in Michigan driving cars. *Mode* brought our paths together. She is a woman whom I greatly admire for not letting a career opportunity of a lifetime pass her by, and for always managing to smile through the struggle of her long-distance engagement.

BARBARA'S STORY

For me, my childhood represented an uneasy partnership of being gifted and feeling self-conscious of my body. Ultimately, it led me to feel undeserving of all that I was good at, because I didn't feel good about myself. I was an accomplished kid at school. What you'd call an athletic child. Being tall, I was good at basketball, and being fast, I beat the boys at sprints. But I'll never forget seeing my fifth-grade photographs, taken at the beginning of the school year. I had just started developing. Just a little, and at the same time just enough to start feeling awkward about my body. I remember looking at the other kids' pictures and comparing myself to them. God, I thought as I looked down at my reflection, I don't like the way I look.

Years later, on a sun-kissed beach in the Bahamas, I felt the same way as the day I saw those photos. I was with Michele that day and I was being photographed for a summer issue of *Mode*. The only thing I had to wear was a swimsuit and a smile. I turned to her as the photographer had finished setting up his equipment, and I said, "I just don't deserve to be here." Michele took me over to a full-length mirror and replied, "Barbara Brickner, you look at yourself. What makes you think you don't deserve to be what all of us see in you?" I didn't have an answer, for I could only see the reflection of a girl posing for her school picture. She continued: "You're here because we see the beauty in you. Not just the curves, the beautiful body, or the beautiful face, but it's what comes out of you." I was awakened. I realized there and then that my mind had taken me back to the day I saw those fifth-grade photographs. It had brought back the same feelings of undeservedness and self-consciousness. That past event had wrapped itself around my current reality. For a brief moment, I believed I was still that schoolgirl.

MY STORY

As a big and shy girl growing up in Southfield, Michigan, my mother believed that I couldn't possibly be happy. Every time I tried to tell her that I was fine, her response was either "Talk to me! Be honest with me!" or "Why can't you be more like your friend Susan?" I was overwhelmed by her persistent questions. I just couldn't get her to listen. True, I wasn't like my closest friend, Susan, who was thinner than I was and also best friends with her mother. I was like *me*.

Convinced that my lack of openness was evidence that I wasn't happy in my bigger body, my mother sent me to see a psychologist. I was eleven.

After school every Thursday, I was forced to share my feelings with a complete stranger who really didn't listen. During my initial visits, I tried to explain to him that I was okay. I had friends, did my homework, and wanted to be an actress. I couldn't see what my mother thought was so terribly wrong with me. His probing questions and dismissive looks made me realize that he thought my mother was right. As the weekly visits went by and I sat on the black leather chair, I, too, began to believe there was something wrong with me. After all, my mother was an adult (and they *always* know more than children) and he was an esteemed professional with certificates and degrees framed on his office wall to prove it. Though I didn't know what was wrong with me, I knew I certainly couldn't be right. To keep them from gathering any further evidence of the offense that I didn't know I had committed, my defense was to withdraw. I grew silent.

Many years later, I was thrilled to receive an invitation from a top Hollywood TV producer, asking me to meet with her during my upcoming trip to Los Angeles. She wanted to discuss the idea of making a made-for-television movie about a fuller-figured woman. What an honor! Not only was it exciting that Hollywood was waking up to the fact that bigger women *can* play romantic lead roles on TV but it was flattering that *I* was being asked to consult on the project. The producer's desk was strewn with unread manuscripts as I took my seat opposite her. We bandied around ideas, knowing that the most successful movies are often based on classic fairy-tale stories like "Cinderella." I then announced to the group, "What about 'The Ugly Duckling'?" The group fell silent as the producer looked at me straight in the eye. Sarcastically, she yelled, "Who's going to play a *duck?*" I was humiliated. I withdrew. In that moment, I was eleven years old in the black leather chair in the psychologist's office, again being unheard, saying things that were deemed invalid, and ultimately feeling that there was something wrong with me.

Now it's your turn. I ask you to face your past.

➤ **TUNE IN**

I want you to keep a journal, your Learning Curves journal. Buy a blank book, open to a fresh page, and write your name in it. Keep it private: It is yours and yours alone.

Take a deep breath and close your eyes. Now describe yourself in five adjectives. You know, the negative ones. (Can I give you an example? I worked on a TV segment with a number of women of all shapes and sizes. One model kept asking me of herself, "Where do you want the *fat* girl?")

Choose your own five words that you believe fit you right now. Write them down. Now think back to when you were six, eleven, or sixteen, to your first memories of feeling the same way. What is your most powerful memory of having these negative beliefs about yourself? Write the experience down in detail. How old were you? Whom were you with? Your family? Friends? Who else? What was going on? Were you at school and someone snatched a bag of chips from your hands? Were you in a clothing store and the sales assistant told you there was nothing that would fit you? Paint the picture as richly as possible. What were the sights, sounds, smells, and tastes associated with that event?

By now, you should have conjured up an incredibly "real" image that reflects a belief you have about yourself today: fat, unattractive, unworthy, awkward, lonely. Do you see the connection? Can you see how a past experience has created the present thoughts you have about yourself?

Now what do you do with those thoughts and memories from the past that are still affecting you today? The answer is, *change them.*

➤ LIVE OUT LOUD

I want to share with you a powerful tool that I learned when I was exposed to the wonderful teachings of Louise L. Hay. Louise is a metaphysical teacher and lecturer, and the best-selling author of fifteen books. She has assisted thousands of people in discovering and using the full potential of their own creative powers for personal growth and healing. The technique of positive affirmation has allowed me to replace the negative beliefs that I had about myself with new, empowering thoughts that have helped me to change my life.

This is one of the simplest and most effective techniques you can use. Like you, I'm sure, I had heard about positive affirmation long before I had read Louise's book *You Can Heal Your Life* (Carlsbad, CA: Hay House, 1984). But the thought of saying oh so nice things about myself under my breath or into a mirror at first seemed somewhat strange. Until I read her story about the tomato plant, that is.

> A healthy tomato plant can have over a hundred tomatoes on it. In order to get this tomato plant with all these tomatoes on it, we need to start with a small dried seed. The seed doesn't look like a tomato plant. It sure doesn't taste like a tomato plant. If you didn't know for sure, you would not even believe that it could be a tomato plant. However, let's say you plant this seed in fertile soil, and you water it and let the sun shine on it.
>
> When the first little tiny shoot comes up, you don't stomp on it and say, "That's not a tomato plant." Rather, you look at it and say, "Oh boy! Here it comes," and you watch it grow with delight. In time, if you continue to water it and give it sunshine and pull away any weeds, you might have a tomato plant with more than a hundred luscious tomatoes. It all began with that one tiny seed.

It is the same with creating a new experience for yourself. The soil you plant in is your subconscious mind. The seed is the new affirmation. *The whole new experience is in the tiny seed.* You water it with affirmations. You let the sunshine of positive thoughts beam on it. You weed the garden by pulling out the negative thoughts that come up. And when you first see the tiniest little evidence, you don't stomp on it and say, "That's not enough!" Instead, you look at this first breakthrough and exclaim with glee, "Oh boy! Here it comes! It's working!"

Then you watch it grow and become the manifestation of your desire.

It's time to plant your seed. Take the list of the negative beliefs you have about yourself. Take each one and turn it into a positive affirmation. Write them down in your journal.

e x a m p l e

Negative belief: **I am undesirable.**

Positive affirmation: **I feel beautiful.**

Make a commitment to yourself to say them every day. At the very least, say your positive affirmations every morning in the bathroom mirror and each night before bed. Use them to combat a negative thought anytime you have one. Say them as often as you can. This is your mantra.

I affirm how wonderful, powerful, honest, beautiful, and joyful I am all the time. I sing these words out loud in the shower, think them as I walk to and from work, and write them in my journal every day. You can use yours anywhere. I take every chance I get to fill my head with positive and empowering thoughts. Do the same for at least one month. Don't give up. Take the action. I promise that over time the negative beliefs you have about yourself will begin to fade.

Every one of your feelings has come from somewhere, be it from someone or something. But they were yesterday's feelings. That's where they should remain. Hold this new truth as your only truth: The past is history and the present is the only thing that creates the world you inhabit right now.

YOU CAN'T CONTROL EVERY SITUATION IN LIFE, BUT YOU CAN CONTROL YOUR RESPONSES TO THEM

Now that you are learning how your past defines your present, you are ready to take the next important step along the learning curve: to remember that your thoughts are created, controlled, and changed by you. You are the guard, the keeper of your thoughts. This is powerful. Take a moment to think about what I'm saying. No experience or situation has to be a negative one. Unless you choose to see it that way. You can't control every situation in life, but you can control the way you respond to them. You need to be careful that you don't allow current situations and experiences to plant the seeds of new negative beliefs.

You can choose to see life's experiences in one of two ways. You may believe that these things have hurt you or you can believe these very things helped to make you who you are today. You have the choice.

Sometimes, what we see as a criticism or judgment isn't that at all. Recently, Dee Dee rejected a passerby's comment: "You go to the gym, girl!" Instead of feeling insulted, she realized that there was another way to hear him: He might be a gym trainer and applauding Dee Dee's decision to exercise by saying, "You go, girl!" Years ago, a female customer in a clothing store where I was shopping said to me as I came out of the fitting room in an oversized shirt, "You're not really going to buy that, are you?" Hurt, I responded, "Did I really ask you?" I took her to mean, Why are you bothering? Nothing you wear is going to make a difference because you're so big. Our tendency is to take people's comments and questions as insults, or, worse, as the truth. Let's look again. The woman who asked me that question may have been thinking, Why are you wearing something so loose when something more fitted would be much more flattering to your figure?

So I ask you this: Is it possible that you could see something that happened to you in a different way?

Remember, your thoughts are a reflection of how you feel about yourself. Sometimes comments that we perceive as being negatively meant seem so only because we interpret them that way. By controlling your thoughts, you create your own reality. Here's how Barbara, Dee Dee, Allison, and I have occasionally been held hostage by our thoughts and how we changed them to create a new reality.

BARBARA'S STORY

Six years ago, a model scout spotted me in Washington. He approached me and asked me, "Have you considered plus-size modeling?" I was so offended. I had never even heard of plus-size modeling. I thought he was sending me the message that my body was unacceptable. He was extremely rude. So I got in my car, found a McDonald's drive-through, and ordered a large fries and a chocolate shake. I said to myself, Okay, honey, if you want fat, I'll give you fat!

Halfway through my fries, I started thinking that maybe his question had been a compliment. By seeing it differently, I opened up to a new possibility. Soon after, I found a modeling agency and began a very happy career. When I look at my life now, I see that I am blessed with a big bottom and big breasts, a beautiful husband, and a job I adore. I think my life would have turned out very differently if I had remained a prisoner of my thoughts.

ALLISON'S STORY

My whole life, I've hated my rapists for violently taking away my virginity and with it my childhood. My body was held hostage at twelve, and my thoughts—filled with resentment and anger—have kept me a prisoner ever since. A while ago, I found myself standing next to a nun in a museum. We were both looking at a painting depicting a rape scene. As we contemplated the picture, I suddenly felt compelled to tell her what had happened to me in the kids' house of my hometown. The urge felt like going to confession. She listened silently. After a few moments, she turned to me and asked me one question that has changed my life. "Have you ever thought about the experience for the rapists? Because in acting the way they did, they have separated themselves from God, lost their integrity, and yet still they walk this earth." I was dumbfounded. All I had ever thought about was what *I* had lost, and I had hated them for it. Her words made me realize the terror of the terrorists, the abuse suffered by the abusers, and the torment of my tormentors. I then actually began to feel some compassion for them. I realize now how horrific their childhoods must have been and how much worse their adulthoods are now.

DEE DEE'S STORY

When I was nineteen, I wrote my dad a letter asking for a loan to buy a car. He always seemed to be resentful when it came to money. Since our relationship consisted mostly of monthly checks and holiday money, it was the only thing I felt comfortable asking him for. Asking for money was really a metaphor for asking for love. I got no reply. When I didn't hear from him, I was devastated. I thought he didn't care about me. It took a while for me to realize that perhaps he was giving me the opportunity to do something for myself. I found a job, saved up money, and bought myself my very first car. It was my new thought of having the courage to stand on my own two feet that gave me what I wanted. And, you know what? Doing it for myself felt so much better.

MY STORY

In college, I received a note from a professor I adored. I did everything he asked: cut my hair, stopped wearing shoulder pads that made me look like a linebacker, and always believed his advice was the truth. I had learned that my beliefs, the way I saw things, were not to be trusted. I had enough evidence from both my mother and my psychologist to support this. My alternative was to leave my decisions in other people's hands. One day, my most treasured acting coach had pinned this note for me on the school hallway bulletin board.

I just get angry when I look at you. I really want to say to you that you should not take acting studio again unless you do something about yourself. No amount of concentration is going to take away from that physical appearance, which destroys everything you do.

I couldn't catch my breath as I walked to my car from the theater with the note in hand. I got into my car and stared in the rearview mirror, wondering how he could be so cruel. Didn't he see the young impressionable woman in front of him who had just delivered Ophelia's final monologue in *Hamlet* before her death? I felt so small and at the same time so huge. The following week, I made sure that I was far away from his gaze in class. I sat at the back and chose to perform only scenes where I wouldn't be the young pretty one. I sold out. I did not honor myself.

He asked me to stay behind after the last class of the semester. "Why have you been so distant and aloof?" he asked. I pulled that note out from my binder and showed him what he had written. He looked at me. I looked at him and tears fell. Thankfully, I summoned the courage to tell him what I believed was the truth. I told him that he didn't have the right to say that my size was more important than my talent. In that moment, I had reclaimed some part of me by standing up for myself, my beliefs, and in what body I choose to live my life. My courage to trust myself paid off. He actually listened.

Take control of your thoughts.

➤ TUNE IN

I'd like you to remember the times when people have said something to your face that you took as an insult. How did you react? How did those comments make you feel?

In your Learning Curves journal, write down the remarks that are the most painful for you. On the opposite side of the page, write down another way that you could have interpreted those comments. Even if their intention was negatively meant, as in my story, in what way did it contribute positively to your growth? For example, did you become stronger, more forgiving, or open your eyes to your own feelings of inadequacy?

➤ LIVE OUT LOUD

Remember, you can't control every situation in life, but you can control your responses to them. This technique shows you how to free yourself from being at the mercy of others' comments. Every night for the next week, look at the day that has passed. In your journal, write down the situations and the comments you took as hurtful.

take these steps:

1. Remember the comment or situation.
2. Recall your reaction to the comment or situation.

now ask yourself:

3. Is it possible that this comment or action was not negatively meant? Was seeing it as negative only my way of interpreting the situation?
4. How could I have interpreted the comment or situation differently or how could I have reacted differently?
5. Was I unclear what was meant by the comment or action, and if so, what could I have done to clarify it at the time?
6. If the comment or action was clearly negatively meant, in what way did it contribute to me positively?

EXAMPLE 1

monday

1. I was at dinner with a large group of people and we started to order. When it came my turn, I ordered an appetizer as well as a main course. The waiter said to me, "You want both?"

2. I responded tersely, "What does it matter to you?"

3. Upon reflection, it is possible that the waiter didn't mean it negatively, but I'm not sure because I didn't ask. My immediate response was to take offense.

4. The waiter could possibly have been asking if I wanted both because he felt they weren't complementary dishes, and he could have been offering to make a better suggestion.

5. I was unclear what he meant by the question, and instead of jumping to a negative conclusion, I could have asked him, "Why do you ask?"

6. Because I didn't seek to clarify his comment, I'm not sure how it was meant.

EXAMPLE 2

tuesday

1. I was taking the bus to work, and I found a seat. After a few stops, the bus was full. A man got on and stood holding on to the pole in front of me because there were no seats left. He looked down at me with disgust and asked, "What business do you have taking up more than one seat?"

2. I felt hurt and angry, and I said, "Screw you!"

3. It was clearly a mean comment.

4. There was no other way to interpret his comment, but I could have said, "That was a pretty unkind remark you just made."

5. It was clear.

6. I realize his comment was meant to be hurtful. My angry reaction clearly let him know he'd succeeded in hurting my feelings. I felt power-less against his comment. This situation gave me an opportunity to learn how to be more powerful in these types of situations. Instead of react-ing by saying, "Screw you," I could have offered a more empowering response simply by saying, "That was a pretty unconscious remark you just made." This response would have allowed me to defend myself without returning his comment with equal disdain. He also wouldn't have been given the satisfaction of knowing that he had really hurt my feelings and I would have felt better that I hadn't sunk to his level. I could have left a bad situation feeling good about the way I'd handled it.

Continue this process. Over time, you will begin to see that offense was often taken when there was no need. In other cases, you'll learn how to respond in a way that's more empowering for you. You'll also discover that the most negative situations no longer have power over you. Soon, these steps won't be an exercise you do at home in your journal; they will be the way you respond in everyday life. Realize that you are always in control.

Take a deep breath and remember the truth. Never give the power of your thoughts over to someone else's ignorance.

The power that our thoughts have over us is immense. But our power to change them in the flick of a switch is much greater. Still, you have to want to change your thoughts about yourself in order to take charge of them. Sometimes it's so easy to cry "victim." Try not to consider yourself the victim in *any* situation. If you consider that those experiences happen so that you can become stronger and more in control, then you can use even the toughest situations to help you become more of who you really want to be.

FORGIVENESS IS AN ACT OF SELF-LOVE

Are you beginning to realize that the experiences that have happened in your life and the way you respond to them have had a great effect on you? You've begun to view the experiences differently, but chances are that you're still angry with the people you've felt have hurt you. This anger is justified. But let me clue you into something: Your feelings of anger and hurt probably have very little effect on those people. They do, however, have a profound effect on you, by keeping you attached to the past and those hurtful experiences. It's all very well you pointing out who's hurt me, you might be thinking, but what do I do about the people that I'm still angry with? Here's my answer: I ask you to forgive them. I know how hard this is. Pride, fear, and anger stand in your way. Each of these feelings is an obstacle that takes an enormous amount of courage to overcome. Do not think that forgiveness is a benevolent and selfless act. It's one of the most liberating things you can do for yourself.

Here's how some of our friends forgave their former ghosts.

DEE DEE'S STORY

My torment by my father led to no further contact with him for the next fourteen years. Yet still I felt his presence in my life. He was with me, in my head, every day. What I did, at twenty-seven years old, was to write a letter of forgiveness to him. This is what I wrote:

You are probably wondering why I am choosing now as the time to finally reach you. All I know is that if I don't, then I will never be able to move on and heal from the deep wounds inflicted upon me as a child. I realize that some of my words may not make sense or they may hurt you, but I am willing to take that chance in order for you to have a deeper understanding of my feelings.

I don't know if you can ever know or acknowledge the extent of damage that your obsession with weight has caused me. Please know that this letter is not intended to blame you for anything, only to make you understand. When you weighed me and screamed at me in your office that day, I was given the message that there was something wrong with me; I wasn't like other people.

As a thirteen-year-old desperate for her daddy's approval, I had no way of defending myself. When I spoke to you periodically throughout my teens, one of the first things you would ask me was, "How's your weight?" Now that I'm an adult, I try to imagine what was going through your head. What I come up with was that you were only trying to help. Believe me, I know this. I suppose you did the best you could and I guess you felt you were doing something unpleasant but necessary in your mind. Well, that is what I am doing now. My intention is that this letter is healing and eye-opening, and not damaging.

I feel sorry and saddened by the fact that you measure yourself and others' self-worth by a number on a scale.

I have devoted so much of my life's energy to hating you and I am simply tired of it. I can't go on like this anymore. I don't hate you. There is still a part of that little girl inside of me who needs her daddy's love.

I got married earlier this year. I am sorry that I was not able to let you know or invite you. I was not ready. I thank God every day for my husband, Ramsey. He is the kindest, most loving, thoughtful, and giving man and I cherish him deeply. And he treats me like I am the most beautiful person he has ever known.

It has taken an extreme amount of work to accept the fact that this person could love me no matter what. I am truly blessed.

My true and honest intention with this letter is to try and make you aware of how the past has shaped the present with regards to how I view myself and our relationship. Now that I am able to share it with you, I hopefully can gain closure on the past and move on.

I also want you to know that I forgive you for everything.

I don't expect you to respond to this letter. Regardless, it needed to be written so that I may find peace within myself.

I am very fortunate to be surrounded by people who love me no matter what I weigh and my sincerest wish is that you may find acceptance of yourself.

Your daughter,

Dee Dee

Forgiveness is an extremely powerful tool in the step toward freedom. After writing her forgiveness letter, Dee Dee describes feeling figuratively lighter. She had finally released the weight of her father's torment, which she had been carrying around with her. She felt proud of herself for writing the letter and powerful for confronting the thoughts in her head. Remember, forgiving another is not giving away your power; it's giving it back to you.

BARBARA'S STORY

I am still getting a handle on the tapes that continue to play in my head. Though the pain of feeling unacceptable has gone, I still don't know if I can wrap my arms around myself. I would say I'm halfway there. I am learning that it's me who has to accept me, and that's a struggle. When I'm hard on myself, I remind myself where I am today and how far I've come. I focus on my life as it is now and I'm left feeling blessed that I have so much: a great husband, a wonderful family, and true friends. I realize that I'm not the girl in high school and I'm working on forgetting the comments that have haunted me.

Healing takes many forms. In Allison's case, healing didn't begin with a pen, but took the form of a journey with her camera.

ALLISON'S STORY

Two years ago, I took a trip back to my hometown. I had not been there for more than twenty years. I arrived and stood outside the house in which I had been raped. A new family lived there now. I started taking pictures with my camera. As I photographed the front of the house, an elderly woman opened the front door. I didn't recognize her and she did not know me. After introducing myself, we chatted for a moment and I felt that she sensed a reason for my being there. That there was something I had to resolve. She asked me, "Allison, would you like to come into the house?" I took a deep breath, knowing that that was my reason for coming, and I followed her inside. She showed me the downstairs, newly painted and very different from how I remembered it. I was allowed to look in every room. Then the woman led me upstairs and into the hallway. I looked around silently. I was struck by the number of family photographs that lined the hallway. Happy children's faces. I suddenly remembered how there weren't any photographs of the boys who raped me when they lived in that house. It seemed strange to me that I could remember such a detail. But I realized that the lack of photographs in the "old house" symbolized a lack of love those boys received. Could those boys have been abused by their parents just as I had been abused by them? They may well have been. I stood there calmly. And in that moment, I forgave them.

I wonder if those men realize there is an emotional, psychological, and spiritual cost to them raping me? What is the price they pay? This past summer, I made a movie in which a woman was raped. I filmed it in that very house. I continue to share my experience in women's groups, but what good does it do if we don't talk to men about rape? The movie was shown from the rapist's perspective. This is how I have healed, and still am healing, myself. And I forgive myself for not realizing throughout adolescence that I needed my body at that weight because it helped to protect me from the unbearable pain.

Sometimes it takes a journey back in time to heal the pain of the past and recognize that you've moved on, to a different town, to another life, to help you lay those ghosts to rest. But remember, it's so important to forgive those closest to you.

MY STORY

What I thought would be a quick chat with my mother turned out to be a conversation that we both will never forget. I had called to tell her that an agent was interested in taking me on as a client. Her first words to me were, "Congratulations, Michele!" Then, in her usual fashion, she went on to add, "Do you have to lose weight?" My whole system of protecting myself had evolved from being silent as she spoke to going the other way and getting angry to defend myself. I fought back with stories of other big women who were successful actresses. But this time, through my yelling, I heard something new from her end of the line: silence as she listened to me.

She was genuinely concerned. She voiced her fears that the career I had chosen in theater might be one in which I would have to conform to a standard that I couldn't meet. Ingenue faces have thin bodies. Not mine. It scared my mother that I wouldn't be appreciated for all my talents as much as it scared me. She said that she didn't want me to conform, even though she knew that it was easier to fit in than to fight the current and swim my own course.

It became a phone call of tears. Both mine and hers. Fondly, she started to talk about always knowing that I was different. She reminded me of the time when, as a little girl, I had wanted to take hula lessons instead of ballet because she and my father had brought me back a grass skirt from Hawaii. She remembered my graduation speech from Sunday school, where I stood up and spoke on the subject of interfaith marriages to hundreds in my Jewish congregation. As she spoke, her memories of me were being told with the voice of a mother's pride. She said I was special. For the very first time, I realized that even though her actions were often hurtful, her intention was to help. I could now see that she had always felt that she was not my enemy, but my supporter and champion. For all of her mistakes, I realized how lucky I was that she cared so much to want to make life easier for me. I wasn't the daughter she had envisioned having: the "married with family," thin daughter who lives close enough that she can see her often and the one who shares her innermost secrets. No, I was the daughter she was proud to say she had. I cried.

And in that moment, I said three words that I never felt I would say to her: "I forgive you."

Today, we speak to each other on the phone all the time. We still have opposing points of view, and I feel that she sometimes wishes that I would do things differently. But beneath her complaints lie genuine concern and love. She listens to what I have to say and respects that I have to find my own way.

Forgiveness is healing. It's a love you give to yourself. It's really important to forgive yourself before you can forgive others. Many of us hold on to the hurtful feelings or experiences in order to validate the pain we feel. The protective shields we build around us is harmful because the torment stays in our heads, defended by anger and fear. Letters are a great way to heal yourself and forgive the people in your past. Sharing your feelings helps you to heal.

Take a deep breath and forgive.

➤ TUNE IN

Think about the people in your past who—consciously or unconsciously—fed your negative self-image. In your Learning Curves journal, make a list, in order of importance, of all the people you are still angry at. Does this include yourself? Ask yourself, Whom am I the most angry at? Now that you know the ghosts in your closet, name by name, it's time for you to forgive them. In your journal, answer these six questions and insert the name of the person you seek to forgive.

ask yourself:

1. Why are you angry with _____ ?

2. What has _____ done to you?

3. What did _____ say to you?

4. How have _____'s words and/or actions affected your life negatively?

5. What positive lessons have you learned from what _____ did to you?

6. Are you ready to forgive _____ ?

➤ LIVE OUT LOUD

I'd like you to pick one person on your list and write a letter of forgiveness. Make sure your letter comes from your heart. Write down everything you wish to express, leave out nothing that still causes you pain, and find a place in your heart that enables you to say, "I forgive you." Seal it and file it away just for you.

It's important only for you to know that you have forgiven someone in your heart of hearts. Your motivation for writing should be to heal your hurt. Should you decide to send it, be absolutely sure that you are not expecting a response. If you do, you're not truly empowering yourself. Dee Dee's letter was sent in early December, and now in March, at the time this book is being written, she has not received a reply. She did not expect one. She didn't need one. She has claimed her own freedom from the past. So can you.

I hope you are discovering how liberating it is to release your past. By confronting the past and healing yourself, you are learning to create new thoughts and positive experiences. You are moving yourself into the present. Remember, forgiveness creates strength. You've just taken the first step to living your life in full.

Step 2

Your Inner Style

So many people walk around without knowing who they are and what they are and want to be. As long as you are searching, you are on the path. Dare yourself to step on the path. Be brave and take that step.

KIM COLES, ACTOR AND AUTHOR

THE JOURNEY INWARD LEADS TO THE GREATEST DISCOVERY—WHO YOU ARE

Now that you've looked in the back of your closet and have thrown out all those old "clothes" that no longer fit, it's time to take a look at the top shelves. By that, I mean your highest self, who you are and want to become in order for you to experience your true self fully. You may already think you know who you are. Ask yourself, Do I really know or do I just know who I am supposed to be?

The dictionary definition of the word *style* is "a manner of doing or being." I'll bet you think that style only applies to the clothes you buy and the women in *Vogue.* Well, it doesn't. I learned about style in its truest sense at, of all places, a memorial service.

Several years ago, someone in the fashion industry who changed the course of my role in the business died of cancer. Funerals are not what we would call the happiest of circumstances. What I find interesting about funerals is that when we mourn the loss of a friend, relative, or mentor, we remember and celebrate the essence of the person who passed on. A fragrance so strong, a perfume so sweet, we are left with the potent memory of who they were. *This* is style. On the front page of the ceremony program, a poem by Maya Angelou paid tribute. Her words touched me more deeply than I can describe with my own. The poem, from *The Collected Poems of Maya Angelou* (New York: Random House, 1994), is called "Phenomenal Woman."

Pretty woman wonder where my secret lies.
I'm not cute or built to model size
But when I start to tell them,
They think I'm telling lies.
I say,
It's in the curve of my arms,
The span of my hips,
The stride of my step,
The curl of my lips.
I'm a woman
Phenomenally.
Phenomenal woman,
That's me.

I walk into a room,
Just as cool as you please,
And to a man,
The fellows stand or
Fall at my knees.
They swarm around me,
A hive of honey bees.
I say,
It's the fire in my eyes,
And the flash of my teeth,
The swing in my waist,
And the joy in my feet.
I'm a woman
Phenomenally.
Phenomenal woman,
That's me.

Men themselves have wondered
What they see in me
They try so much
But they can't touch
My inner mystery.
When I try to show them,
They say they still can't see.
I say,
It's in the arch of my back,
The sun of my smile,
The ride of my breasts,
The grace of my style.
I'm a woman
Phenomenally.
Phenomenal woman,
That's me.

Now you understand
Just why my head's not bowed.
I don't shout or jump about
Or have to talk real loud.
When you see me passing,
It ought to make you proud.
I say,
It's in the click of my heels,
The bend of my hair,
The palm of my hand,
The need for my care.
'Cause I'm a woman. Phenomenally.
Phenomenal woman, that's me.

I was moved to tears after reading the poem. What a "phenomenal" way to be remembered. To have been. Often, when I think about who I am, it comes out in a sob. I, like you, have held back so much of myself because I think the world can handle only a certain amount or that I won't be accepted if I'm not what others think I should be. But there are people who love you unconditionally. My friends Julianne and Joyce are both women who feel this way about me. They are people who see beyond what I see in my moments of doubt. I look for friends who can give me the support and the strength to feel good about myself and be true to who I am. These two women are my best mirrors for always seeing me as I am. For instance, when I decided to write this book and it was accepted by a publisher, Julianne called me the next day and said, "I am so proud of you." I just cried. As I worked on this book, I realized I am always on a *learning curve.* I am constantly learning who I am and what I stand for. I've spoken about my mother and her belief that happiness is correlated with your size. That is not my belief. She believes we create ourselves from the outside in. I believe we create ourselves from the inside out. We have to ask ourselves, What is the best for me?

Our parents are our guides. They lead us in a certain direction and often want us to take the narrower path. But they are not us. We need to learn to be ourselves. I've learned to respect my mother's views even when I do not share them. But there are things my parents have given me that I wouldn't trade for the world. That is, loyalty, confidence, and the love of art. As much as my mother has been a nemesis to me, she's also been an inspiration. She's always stood by my choices to try new things and challenge the world's beauty myth even though there was great doubt in her own eyes. Right now, as my father's dealing with a brain injury as a result of open-heart surgery, I watch my mother's strength. She is now in her sixties and having to deal with her husband as though he were her child, not her life partner. I am in awe of how she supports my father to be the best that he can be.

In order to find out who you really are, you need to take the journey inward to see if your choices and actions are truly a reflection of your essence or merely the act of fulfilling other people's expectations. Often, many of us don't know the difference between the two. It is especially true for bigger women because so many of us are told from the moment we're deemed fat that we need to be something that we are not. I can now see that my years of dieting didn't come from the "thin" woman inside of me trying to get out, but, rather, from my making choices based on other people's views.

The stories I will share with you, along with my own search for my true self, reveal how important it is to become connected to our essence. My story and those of the two women you will read about in this step relate two very different journeys, but ultimately they had the same purpose: seeking to find our inner style.

I knew Kate Dillon from afar when she was fighting to stay a size-eight model when I was at *Mademoiselle.* But she showed up in my life years later when she found the truth of who she was as a size fourteen. We met after I began working at *Mode.* Kate is my hero. Even though she is one of the greatest faces of our time, it is off-camera that she comes into her own. Kate is the one who loves being a girl with me. We laugh at how crazy most of us are, especially ourselves. Most of all, she has taught me to take risks. She helps young girls confront their eating disorders by speaking at schools with the compassionate voice of someone who's been there herself. We are like sisters. We both stand up for what we believe: trying to set an example for all full-figured women to look and feel beautiful.

KATE'S STORY

I lived the life of a typical New York model. I'd wake up, drink three cups of coffee, pick up the jeans and T-shirt off the bedroom floor, and fly out the door. One day, I arrived late for a catalog shoot. I was being photographed with another girl. In an industrial-looking studio on Manhattan's Lower West Side, I was being fitted, styled, and groomed for my first outfit. A high-volume CD pumped loud dance music at ten in the morning, and the hair and makeup people reflected the upbeat mood. I glanced over at the other girl, already dressed, as my hair was being swept up, and I remember thinking, Why don't I look like her? I began to worry that the photographer and stylists were thinking the same way. The clothes didn't seem to fit me as well as they did the other model, and I could have kicked myself for eating peach cobbler à la mode before bed late the previous night.

After the shoot, I went home, and the red flash of my answering machine signaled a message. It was my booker/business manager. I returned his call. During the conversation, he said to me, "Kate, I've just been looking at old photos of you. You know, you *used* to have an amazing body." He went on to say, "Now you have a good body, but you once had an amazing body. I don't think you're trying to lose weight. I think you're cheating and lazy." I burst into tears as I hung up the phone, realizing that he was expressing how I had felt about myself earlier that day. Crying, I phoned a friend, who consoled me by saying, "You don't have to be a model. No one's holding a gun to your head." Moments later, my booker called me back to apologize, and I found myself laughing hysterically at him. "Thank you," I said, "for making me realize this is over. I am done with modeling."

I packed my bags and left for home in San Diego. I just wanted to be held by my mother. I spent my time hiking and surfing, dancing on empty dance floors and telling boys they were really cute. I'd never done this in New York. For the first time, I felt free. I realized that I didn't have to fit myself into something that I wasn't.

Most of us never stop to ask, Do I really want this? We just march along to the beat of someone else's drummer, never pausing to listen to whether he's playing our tune. Only when you tune in to your own beat can you play *your* song.

ference between the two. It is especially true for bigger women because so many of us are told from the moment we're deemed fat that we need to be something that we are not. I can now see that my years of dieting didn't come from the "thin" woman inside of me trying to get out, but, rather, from my making choices based on other people's views.

The stories I will share with you, along with my own search for my true self, reveal how important it is to become connected to our essence. My story and those of the two women you will read about in this step relate two very different journeys, but ultimately they had the same purpose: seeking to find our inner style.

I knew Kate Dillon from afar when she was fighting to stay a size-eight model when I was at *Mademoiselle.* But she showed up in my life years later when she found the truth of who she was as a size fourteen. We met after I began working at *Mode.* Kate is my hero. Even though she is one of the greatest faces of our time, it is off-camera that she comes into her own. Kate is the one who loves being a girl with me. We laugh at how crazy most of us are, especially ourselves. Most of all, she has taught me to take risks. She helps young girls confront their eating disorders by speaking at schools with the compassionate voice of someone who's been there herself. We are like sisters. We both stand up for what we believe: trying to set an example for all full-figured women to look and feel beautiful.

KATE'S STORY

I lived the life of a typical New York model. I'd wake up, drink three cups of coffee, pick up the jeans and T-shirt off the bedroom floor, and fly out the door. One day, I arrived late for a catalog shoot. I was being photographed with another girl. In an industrial-looking studio on Manhattan's Lower West Side, I was being fitted, styled, and groomed for my first outfit. A high-volume CD pumped loud dance music at ten in the morning, and the hair and makeup people reflected the upbeat mood. I glanced over at the other girl, already dressed, as my hair was being swept up, and I remember thinking, Why don't I look like her? I began to worry that the photographer and stylists were thinking the same way. The clothes didn't seem to fit me as well as they did the other model, and I could have kicked myself for eating peach cobbler à la mode before bed late the previous night.

After the shoot, I went home, and the red flash of my answering machine signaled a message. It was my booker/business manager. I returned his call. During the conversation, he said to me, "Kate, I've just been looking at old photos of you. You know, you *used* to have an amazing body." He went on to say, "Now you have a good body, but you once had an amazing body. I don't think you're trying to lose weight. I think you're cheating and lazy." I burst into tears as I hung up the phone, realizing that he was expressing how I had felt about myself earlier that day. Crying, I phoned a friend, who consoled me by saying, "You don't have to be a model. No one's holding a gun to your head." Moments later, my booker called me back to apologize, and I found myself laughing hysterically at him. "Thank you," I said, "for making me realize this is over. I am done with modeling."

I packed my bags and left for home in San Diego. I just wanted to be held by my mother. I spent my time hiking and surfing, dancing on empty dance floors and telling boys they were really cute. I'd never done this in New York. For the first time, I felt free. I realized that I didn't have to fit myself into something that I wasn't.

Most of us never stop to ask, Do I really want this? We just march along to the beat of someone else's drummer, never pausing to listen to whether he's playing our tune. Only when you tune in to your own beat can you play *your* song.

I had been watching Kim Coles on television as Synclaire, the role she played in *Living Single.* It wasn't until I saw Kim perform her Off-Broadway play, *Homework,* in New York a few years ago that I saw her ability to share her inner beauty through humor. She loves fashion and now hosts segments on cable TV's *New Attitudes.* (I had a guest spot last year to share my personal closet tips!) Kim even found time in her hectic filming schedule to write a humorous anecdotal book, *"I'm Free, but It'll Cost You,"* which sheds light on dating, sex, and relationships as a full-figured woman.

KIM'S STORY

Once I figured out who I was, that's how I was seen. Our high school years are so important. Everyone has a label in school. There's "the pretty one," "the bad one," "the smart one," "the athletic one," and "the girl who sits alone for lunch." I thought that I was "the fat one" until one day at school, having watched the miniseries *Roots* the night before, I humorously mimicked the characters in the show. I gathered quite an audience, who watched my rendition. They laughed hysterically. It was then that I realized that I was "the funny one." That's who I was. Who I am. My first thought about myself became "funny," not "fat." Consequently, I never experienced "the fat girl story" in school. You know, no dates, no fun. I was on the cheering squad, dated two football players (not at the same time), had great friends, joined the drama club, and was elected class president four years in a row. I look back and realize that I showed my friends something inside me. My philosophy today is the same: You can call me fat if you want to, but fat is not all I am.

MY STORY

One of the hardest decisions I've ever had to make was to leave the theater. I had grown sick and tired of playing matrons, mothers, elderly aunts, and cameo big girls. I knew that I had talent, a talent confirmed by my teachers and friends. Destined, I thought, to play the leading role and not an extra in the chorus. I believed I was supposed to play Romeo's Juliet and not her mother, Lady Capulet. I thought I was Medea. She was fiery and passionate, and she never compromised who she was in an attempt to conform.

Weeks before auditioning for the part of Medea, I had learned all her lines by heart. I was Medea in the hallways, Medea in the evenings, Medea on the weekend. When the day arrived, I had nailed down every scene perfectly. Nervously, I took off with the play in hand. I took several deep breaths as I stood outside the theater doors and the director's assistant summoned me in. He told me to take the stage. I remember the director sitting in the middle of the auditorium with his legs thrown over the chair in front of him. He told me which scene I was to recite, and, without hesitation, I began. Medea poured out from every pore of my skin, every vein in my body. I said my last line and stood in a buzz of silence—a long silence. Still with his legs slumped in the same position, motionless, the director finally spoke. "You need to lose fifty pounds or wait fifteen years if you want to get another role."

I stood stunned, like someone who'd just been in an accident. I said nothing in reply, but I found enough courage to walk off the stage and back outside. I felt utterly humiliated. On my way home, I decided that I had just taken my final bow. You see, if I could not play the roles I wanted, how would I be happy in a career playing only sidekick roles? No more cameos, no more chorus, no more theater.

I was more than "just a pretty face," and if college professors and casting directors couldn't see past that, then they were missing a big piece of me. I was frustrated by being unable to perform as an actor on my terms. What I did was lift myself off the floor on which my self-esteem had been trampled and start again. With all the steps I took backward—answering phones at Perry Ellis, photocopying sketches at Anne Klein, and selling costume jewelry at Bloomingdale's—I made one giant leap forward. What I found was that, without question, I loved fashion and design. And into the fashion world I fell.

The search for your inner style begins by developing a relationship with yourself.

Tune in to your inner voice, your essence.

➤ TUNE IN

Close your eyes. I want you to imagine that you're at your funeral. Imagine that you are a fly on the wall, or that you're floating unseen above everyone gathered in the room. Look down. Whom do you see? Friends, family, the people who loved you the most. One by one, each person gets up to share his or her remembrance of you. They speak of all the things that they loved the most about you: your kindness, sincerity, creativity, the way you helped others, and the way you smiled. Listen carefully. This is who you are. This is why they loved you.

Most likely, these remembrances didn't include your dress size or how big your thighs were. They celebrated the real you. Now write down the experience in detail. What did each person say about you? Did these qualities and ways of being sound familiar, or were they things that you had discounted as unimportant?

➤ LIVE OUT LOUD

This exercise will allow you to see what people treasure about you. This is your essence.

Take a look at how much of your real self you've expressed. Reread what you've written. Take what each person has said about you and edit it to just a few words that capture the essence of what he or she said. List them. This list reflects the qualities that are at the core of your essence. Now make four columns on a fresh page in your journal and write the headings below. Go through all the qualities on the list and put an *X* next to the quality in the relevant column.

EXAMPLE

QUALITY	I EMBODY THIS ALL THE TIME	SOME OF THE TIME	VERY RARELY
Sincere		✔	
Enthusiastic	✔		
Loving		✔	
Ability to laugh at myself			✔

Can you see that there are wonderful qualities you possess that you have kept hidden in the shadows? Allow them to come to the surface. Allow the real you to emerge. Choose one quality to work on that's not as developed in you as you'd like. In your Learning Curves journal each evening, look back at that day.

a s k   y o u r s e l f :

1. Was this quality of mine evident today?

2. If so, how?

3. How did it make me feel to embody this quality?

4. What were people's responses (if any) to me exemplifying this quality?

5. Did this feel like a natural expression of who I am or want to become more of?

6. Do I see the benefit of consciously trying to embody this quality?

7. If the quality was not in evidence today, were there opportunities in which I could have embodied this quality? List them.

8. If I had embodied this quality, would it have made my day more fulfilling?

9. Do I see the value in consciously trying to embody this quality?

Work on one quality at a time until you feel that you embody that quality naturally in your everyday life. Then focus on the next quality.

Sometimes others can see wonderful things about you that you often overlook as unimportant. You may find that very little of your energy has been focused on letting your true self shine through. Instead, you have often put your energy in trying to be something you're not. The act of consciously looking at your behavior will help to reveal the woman you are.

LEARNING CURVE 5

GIVING UP THE FANTASY ALLOWS YOU TO LIVE YOUR REALITY

The journey to find your true self is not always an easy road. Not only are we influenced by our family's desires and opinions but almost every moment of every day we are confronted with seductive messages that promise the keys to happiness.

Malls full of stores with things we think we need, movies with plotlines we think our lives should follow, and images in fashion magazines of what we think we should look like. Almost every message speaks the four-letter word: *thin.*

Most of our efforts to measure up to society include the requisite attempts to reach the right number on the scale. Because few full-figured women have had permanent "success" in this area, we often find ourselves expending an enormous amount of energy to fulfill society's other ideals.

KIM'S STORY

I have lived in Hollywood as an actress for the last ten years. Being funny paid off. I was hired to perform in a sitcom called *In Living Color.* I was happy for a while, driving to the studio and decorating my trailer. Two years after I left the show, I joined the cast of *Living Single.* But over four years I gained fifty pounds. I injured my knees in an effort to exercise like a demon to lose the weight and had to have two knee surgeries in three years. I refused to subject myself and the cast to "fat girl" jokes in the script. So I was fired. Several months later, I attended a Hollywood party. How fabulous, you may think. Gorgeous, glamorous, famous people sipping champagne and talking about movies. Not quite.

During the party, a woman approached me and said, "Didn't you used to be Kim Coles?" My first response was to slap her. I didn't, because a millisecond later I found myself feeling sorry for her. Sad that this woman could define me only if I was on her little idiot box every Thursday. Even sadder that she felt I was only valid to her as the person she saw on TV. My answer to her question was this: "I am Kim Coles whether I'm a big star or whether

I'm sitting around scratching my ass!" I realized that I am Kim Coles no matter what I'm doing. That's a great feeling. I am *in* Hollywood but not *of* it. Most of the people at the party were just exchanging business cards in an effort to find their next job anyway.

Remember, our ego craves others' attention, while our soul seeks only our own. While the ego reacts to experience, the soul creates it. Your ego can live a lie, but only your soul knows your *truth*.

KATE'S STORY

At home with my family, I reminisced about my modeling days in New York. I'd been hanging out with the coolest people in the city, had a great apartment in the heart of Manhattan, traveled the world, and really lived the life. Suddenly, I was fat and waiting tables in San Diego! How did I go from being so "fabulous" to being so not? I met a friend back home who was having more fun than I ever had. It was after talking to her that I saw clearly all the bullshit that surrounded my life in New York. I had been completely sucked into the falseness of the people I associated with, the keeping up appearances I did, and the judgments I had. I realized the lie that I had been living. My modeling days were not "all that." In fact, those days were probably the unhappiest in my life.

MY STORY

Four years down the fashion road, I was a senior editor at *Mademoiselle*. My hard work as an assistant for several years had paid off. I'd made it! I'd arrived! At the European fashion shows, chauffeurs met me at the airport, flowers greeted me in my hotel room, and invitations were showered at my feet. But something still didn't feel quite right. By now, I was thirty, working on a twenty-something magazine, as a size sixteen with a bunch of size sixes. Fitting into fashion was a struggle—literally. I had to figure out what clothes I needed to wear in order to be labeled "cool." The clothes also had to be as flattering as possible so I didn't look "fat": the biggest fashion faux pas. That meant blazers and white shirts and heels that hurt. Not only was it about looking fabulous; it also had to do with where I was "seen." I went to all the parties, surrounded by people I knew by title, not name: the fashion editor of this and the market editor of that. I had to smile at them as though I recognized their "importance," and all the while I tried to figure out what was "in" at that moment: the "hot" music, books, and movies. This gave me something to talk to them about.

During the Paris shows, we all had to sit on little gilt chairs. I would squeeze myself into the seat and sit shoulder-to-shoulder between two skinny ladies. For me, it was the most uncomfortable ordeal. What I thought would be fun felt more like torture. Even though the shows were about fabulous parties, fabulous clothes, and fabulous people, they just left me thinking, How am I going to get into my next seat? And, more importantly, How can I make the fashion world fit me?

It was during one show when yet another skinny model came down the runway to rapturous applause, wearing nothing but a skirt the size of a tube top. I realized that I no longer believed that this could be the only vision of beauty for all women. On the streets and on the subway, I had seen many beautiful women who didn't look like this or the women we featured in *Mademoiselle*. I began to struggle with the idealized notion of beauty. Where did I fit in? I stopped feeling good about the creativity of my work and started feeling bad about the message my work was sending to myself and other women.

I now ask you to face your life as it is today.

➤ **TUNE IN**

Look at the following list. Really think about each area. Ask yourself, Have I made my decisions in these areas of my life based on who I really am and what I want, or to fulfill others' expectations?

	BASED ON MY NEEDS	BASED ON OTHERS' EXPECTATIONS
Home		
Family		
Career		
Relationship with self		
Relationship with others		
Finances		
Social life		
Charity/Contribution		
Spirituality/Religion		
Hobbies/Interests		

now ask yourself:

1. What's keeping me from expressing my true self in the areas where I'm making my decisions based on other people's expectations?

2. Can I see that by making changes in these areas of my life I would be happier and more fulfilled?

➤ LIVE OUT LOUD

The first step in changing anything in your life is being conscious of the fact that there's something you want to change. Now you are going to go on a search to find your own expression in each area of your life, to begin living your life on your terms.

take these steps:

1. Take a trip to your local newsstand or magazine shop. Choose a store that has a large selection of magazines covering a variety of topics. Look for magazines that cover the areas of your life that you want to work on. Don't limit yourself to the magazines you normally read. Buy the ones that catch your eye.

2. Take each area in your life where you're still making choices based on other people's expectations and title the top of one page with a reading for that area in your Learning Curves journal. For example, you may have a page with the heading "Home," and another with "Relationship."

3. Put one hour aside each week when you can have some quiet time alone. Look through the magazines that you bought. Study the pictures while you keep in mind the areas in your life that you are working on. Look for something to inspire or move you. Try to find pictures that help you begin to envision what you might want in these areas of your life.

4. Cut out the images and paste them on the appropriate page of your journal. Begin to create a collage.

5. Continue this process every week, until you paint a picture of what you want your life to look like in these areas.

6. Look at your collages on a regular basis so you can stay focused on what you want and on what is possible.

Now that you are beginning to learn more about what *you* want, you have turned an important curve on the journey to making it a reality.

You Can't Know Yourself Unless You Spend Time with Yourself

One step that I believe is essential on this journey to know yourself better is really to spend time with yourself. Free from the distractions that you live with daily: the endless "To do" list, "Shoulds," and "Have tos." Close all that off, even for just a few moments, and open up to meditation.

Taking the time to be quiet with ourselves is something we rarely do. But if you don't spend time to be alone with yourself, you are not having a relationship with yourself. You are in the world but not in *your* world. Meditation is an effective way of reconnecting with yourself. I know you immediately have an image of superspiritual people sitting on cushions, eyes shut, legs crossed. I assure you, it's not like that.

The most succinct definition of meditation is provided in the words of Jon Kabat-Zinn in Sarah Ban Breathnach's book *Simple Abundance: A Day Book of Comfort and Joy* (New York: Warner Books, 1995): "Meditation is simply about being yourself and knowing about who that is. It's about coming to realize that you are on a path whether you like it or not, namely the path that is your life."

KATE'S STORY

I walked down the street, thinking that I needed something more in my life. Stopping dead in my tracks, I literally saw a sign. Above me was a poster advertising a karate school. I looked at it for about five minutes and wondered if I would be any good. Modeling was all about perfection, and I viewed karate with the same eyes. Reluctantly, I dared myself to step inside. An instructor, dressed in full karate gear, asked me why I was interested in learning karate. My first reaction was to say that I wanted to show everyone how great I could be at it. There was a big part of me that still felt I had something to prove. Then I realized why I was actually there. I said, "I'm here because I don't want to think about anything but myself for a while." I signed up for my first class later that week.

During the first few classes, I felt self-conscious and bad at karate. I expressed those feelings to someone in my class, who said, "Kate, no one else is as strong, calm, and centered as you." I'll never forget her words of reassurance. I released my fears about not being good enough and started to truly love it. I left the karate class feeling great and had an awareness of myself—my sense of being and my sense of strength. I felt lighter, freer, and happy. Isn't that what you do meditation for?

Learning karate has become my meditation. I've been going to class for four years. Like dancing, you can learn the moves, but you have to feel your soul in order to truly experience yourself.

Often, quiet time means just that. Being alone with yourself doesn't mean staying in and watching television. Far from it. Time with yourself means disconnecting from everything around you, even your thoughts.

KIM'S STORY

I now really enjoy my own company. It's funny—I used to hate being alone. Every time I came home with my entourage of friends, my mother used to tease me by calling me "Boots and her buddies." Now, as an adult, I do meditate in the "classic sense," legs crossed, eyes closed, you know the rest. But nothing gives me a greater sense of myself than a long walk. When I'm walking in Southern California, wherever I'm going, I don't think about anything. I am absent of thought. I let everything wash over me and just listen. I listen to the chirping of the birds, the soft howl of the trees, the wind on my face, and the calm words of the ocean waves. I am totally connected to myself when I take a walk.

MY STORY

A year after being at *Mademoiselle,* the stress of making all the deadlines and keeping up the appearances had made me weary. On my first vacation in years, I decided the best present I could give myself was to go to a spa. I needed to relax. When I arrived at Canyon Ranch in Arizona, I looked at all the classes I could take. Mornings were spent at Sunrise Yoga, afternoons in a class called Chakra Breathing, and early evenings taking Sunset Meditation. I had taken yoga classes back in New York that included a five-minute meditation at the end of Yoga Zone, but I had never committed myself to learning different ways to handle stressful times or even know what the benefits would be.

At the spa, I got the chance to meet a master, Lawrence LeShan, who wrote the definitive book *How to Meditate* (New York: Bantam, 1984). He told me his theory on what the benefits of meditation were. "You have a chance to get to a sense of calm and tranquillity that has you looking at life in a more soulful, connected way." I was spellbound as he spoke, and I soaked up all the different meditation classes like a sponge. I left my week in Tucson relaxed. Not just physically but also mentally. I wanted to function in my hectic life with that kind of peace of mind. But how?

In New York a week later, I had lunch with a friend, Derek Anderson. He looked at me and said he had never seen me so relaxed. As I shared what I had learned on my vacation, he told me about a woman named Patricia Albere. Patricia has been leading motivational groups for the last twenty years. As a spiritual teacher, she conducts individual and group sessions each month in Los Angeles and New York. She teaches classes on the subject of centering and living from one's soul. I began to see her for private sessions and for one weekend every month for the last five years, I do a group "intensive" that is led by her. Fifteen adults from all walks of life: Financial bankers, artists, company directors, psychologists, doctors, and I, the token fashion editor, congregate at a friend's brownstone to meditate together. We share our life experiences and work through exercises similar to the ones in this book. I take myself out of my busy life and experience a sense of feeling grounded. It makes me feel strong enough to handle whatever is going on in the world around me.

Last winter, my grandmother was taken to a hospice. She had been diagnosed with cancer and had little time to live. I would regularly sit alone with my grandmother and read to her from a book called *Tuesdays with Morrie,* a story of a man who visits his dying professor every Tuesday. Like the professor, my grandmother was also struggling with her impending death. Through meditation, I was able to create a clear, calm space inside me that allowed me to listen to her tell me all that she felt—about wanting to die and at the same time trying to live.

During one meditation weekend, I received an urgent phone call from my family. My grandmother had passed away. I don't think I could have handled their pain and my own grief if I hadn't meditated with the people in the group, who have supported me through my toughest challenges. Meditation has made a true difference in my life. It helps me relieve the stress of the world's chaos, gives me the opportunity to check in with my feelings and to stay grounded in whatever's occurring around me. Most importantly, meditation allows me to experience all the grace in my life.

Now it's your turn to reacquaint yourself with your self.

➤ TUNE IN

Think about how meditation will help improve your life. Make a list in your journal. Here are a few ideas to get you started.

1. Gives me time for myself.
2. Makes me feel more relaxed and centered.
3. Gives me greater peace.
4. Enables me to destress.
5. Gives me greater self-control

➤ LIVE OUT LOUD

Following is a step-by-step beginners guide to meditation that has been developed by Bob Rose, the director of the Meditation Society of America. Start out slowly, about ten minutes a day, and build up to longer sessions over time.

1. Set your alarm clock to ring after ten minutes.
2. Sit in a position that is comfortable for you. Make sure your back is upright. Use a cushion to help. If you are uncomfortable sitting, you can lie down flat.
3. Close your eyes.
4. Now relax your body. Do this by working from your toes to your head, tensing each part of your body for ten seconds and then releas-

ing the tension. Do this for each part of your body. Now your body should be physically relaxed.

5. Feel your breath go in and out. As you do this, allow your thoughts to go by like a movie on a screen. Simply observe. If you begin to think about anything for too long—work, the kids—just bring your focus back to your breathing. Let your thoughts fly away.

6. After ten minutes, open your eyes. Write down how you feel in your journal.

7. Be patient! You won't become a master meditator overnight. Keeping focused on your breath may be difficult initially, but with prac-tice, it will become easier and the benefits will be clear.

This is just one way to meditate. As you read in the stories, there are other ways to spend time with yourself. Experiment. Read a book, such as *How to Meditate,* or look into taking a meditation class. Above all, enjoy the experience of quiet time.

LEARNING CURVE 7

YOU HAVE THE POWER TO PLANT THE SEEDS FOR A NEW REALITY

Your essence, like a perfume, is made up of a number of ingredients. No one is one thing, one size, one color, one personality. How boring would the world be then? Now that I hope you are beginning to get a sense (and a scent) of who you are, take the journey with me to express your inner style to the outer world.

KATE'S STORY

My time in San Diego forced me to think about who I was. After months of soul searching, experiencing freedom, and a process I called "radical honesty," I realized something. As much as I loved the peace at home, the feeling of not having to think about my size and weight, and the honesty and connection with real friends, I still yearned to be in New York. The pace, culture, and excitement really suited me. I also realized that I really wanted to be a model. But on *my* terms. In *my* body. I wouldn't have realized this if I had stayed in New York.

Before heading back to New York, I metaphorically rewrote the story of my life: a life that combined the best of both of these worlds and without the parts that no longer fit. My life, free from the expectations of others, one with a fulfilling modeling career, my continued commitment to karate, and a real home in the city. Over the last few years, I have achieved this and more. Renewed in New York, I found a modeling agency that had fuller-figured girls on their books. Today, I work with Michele, who inspires me to feel my most beautiful in the pictures that we take for *Mode,* and with celebrated photographer Richard Avedon to create new ways of advertising plus sizes for stores like the Avenue. I continue to strengthen my body and soul through karate, and I have found a perfect brownstone apartment. I am thankful every day for the life I have now, and for finding out who I really am.

KIM'S STORY

After I was fired from the sitcom *In Living Color* and then began working on *Living Single* until the show stopped taping and went into reruns, I really had to think about what I would do next. I realized that I still loved acting, but there was something inside me that I needed to express. What was it and how would I do it? I had always wanted to write, produce, and star in my own play—a play about me. It was a scary thought because I had never done anything like this before. But every time I thought about doing the play, something stirred inside me. My gut instinct led me to think about making it happen. With a writer friend of mine, we figured out the story. It would revolve around the lives of three best friends, all of whom were aspects of me. I took all my savings and set out to produce the play in New York and L.A. And I did. The play, entitled *Homework,* had nothing to do with my size, gender, race, or profit. In its purest form, the play was about me saying I was going to do something and then proceeding to do it.

MY STORY

In 1993, I left *Mademoiselle.* There had been thirteen upper-management changes in two and a half years. Through the upheaval, a groundbreaking move gave me hope. The first plus-size fashion story was planned. It was shot in Paris but did not make it into the magazine. The reason: It was too extreme. The editor was concerned about what the reaction might be to putting larger women in the pages of the magazine. Disillusioned by the decision to keep the magazine targeted to only women up to size fourteen, I had reached the point where I felt it was time to part ways.

Although I knew that staying at *Mademoiselle* was not the right choice, I didn't know what I would do next. I still loved fashion, and I found work as a freelance editor to pay the rent while I figured out what my next step would be. I had collected hundreds of magazines over the years, and as I reread some of them back at home, it gave me a chance to see what was missing from magazineland.

Surrounded by a stack of old *Vogues*, I took out my journal and wrote a vision for my life. Patricia, my spiritual teacher, had taught me how to write a vision. "Write want you want to manifest in your life in the first person, present tense, as if it were happening right now." This is what I wrote.

We have been working on the creation of a full-figured magazine that enhances self-worth and esteem. And other women are able to gain their full potential as I have with this vision. This creation makes me shine in God's proud gaze for taking a stand for others in this world. We have created a space for grace for all women to heal the wounds of body image, and open the possibility for others to find peace in their souls' truth, beyond the visual. With this magazine, we have opened the door for others like me, who struggle in the world, with a new sense of being held and appreciated as they are.

Being a woman of size and in fashion, I wanted to take all my experience and work on a magazine that spoke to 65 million women in America. Women like me.

Six months after writing this entry and reading it every night before bed, I was introduced to two women who shared my vision and who were in the idea stage of creating a magazine. I found myself part of a team of women who were committed to making this vision take form. It has, in *Mode*. Now, as the fashion and style director, I realize that I am supporting a new concept of beauty and style. I am, in my own way, making a difference and have found a way to express my style.

Now that you are free from the conditioning of others, free from your own beliefs that have held back your inner style for so long, it's time for you to envision your life as you need to in order to express fully who you are.

➤ TUNE IN

Now that you have begun to differentiate between what you really want in life and what you thought you should have, it's time to write a vision for your life.

follow these steps:

1. Take a moment to look at the collages you have made in your Learning Curves journal.

2. Find a quiet place, indoors or out, alone. Leave your journal beside you.

3. Now close your eyes and take several deep breaths.

4. Visualize your life or one area of your life as you want it to be. What's happening on the picture you're painting? Who is with you? What do your surroundings look like? What are you doing? What else do you see? Like an artist at her canvas, paint the mood, detail, feeling. Hold the picture vividly in your head. Perhaps you find yourself smiling at the image you've created. Maybe a sense of awe washes over you as you find yourself excited by the possibility and realize the challenges that await you. Keep your eyes closed for ten minutes.

5. Open them. In your journal, paint the picture in words. Remember as much as possible.

6. Write your vision in the first person, present tense. "I am" or "I have" as if it is happening today. By doing this, you are sending this message out to the universe. On paper, you are bound.

7. Whenever you feel lost or depressed, reread your vision. Use it as your inspiration and guide.

➤ LIVE OUT LOUD

This vision may seem very different from an area in your current life, but it doesn't have to be that way for very long. Use this goal-setting exercise to help you begin making this vision a reality.

take these steps:

1. Select one area of your vision to work on first. For example, changing careers. Realizing that you need to take a course, your first goal may be to research study programs. Do it. Success with the easier goals will allow you to overcome your fears and build confidence. Then you can work up to the bigger challenges on your list.

2. Write what you want to achieve in the form of a goal. Make it clear, measure your progress, and, though it may be difficult, make the goal possible to achieve. For example, your goal is now to enroll in a class.

3. Commit to a date by which you will achieve your goals. Write them down. Do it in the form of a time line.

4. List all the possible benefits you will receive from achieving each goal.

5. List the potential obstacles that may prevent you from achieving each goal and the possible solutions to overcoming these obstacles. This will help you to keep moving toward your goals, instead of giving up when the inevitable roadblocks appear.

6. Continue to chart your progress and keep refining your goals until you have achieved exactly what you want. Your goals may change over time. You may head in one direction, only to find that you actually want to go in another. Don't be hard on yourself. This is all part of the process. What's important is that you are consciously searching to find the life you desire and to achieve *your* goals.

Step 3

Living in Your Skin

It's amazing the lengths we'll go to, to be accepted. The last thing we seem willing to do is accept ourselves. The irony, of course, is that once we do accept ourselves, others accept us. There is nothing so seductive than someone who respects and feels good about herself.

CAMRYN MANHEIM, ACTOR AND AUTHOR

BODY IMAGE IS ALL IN THE MIND

The third essential step to living your life in full and with style takes you on a tour of your body and the feelings you have about it. This is a major learning curve and the exploration will lead you to a wonderful discovery: self-acceptance. On a CBS *48 Hours* segment, "The Price of Perfection" (May 27, 1999), Dan Rather said:

> The number of people who say they are unhappy with the way they look is rising faster than ever. For women, it may be as high as 80 percent. A lot of people who develop illnesses or obsessions about body image say they were relentlessly teased in their youth. Young people especially need to get the message. Self-esteem has to come from inside, not from some trendy standard that few will ever attain. Whatever your age, if you're compromising your health or your happiness, face it. You're paying too high a price for perfection.

The whole subject of the body is what I call the "argument." The argument goes something like this: My body's okay; I'm okay. My body's not okay; I'm not okay. I have had the same argument with my own body. Throughout adolescence, I weighed myself every morning and evening on the scale that was kept in the storage closet at home. As a teenager, I never wanted to talk openly about my body to anyone. Forget it. No, the "argument" could only be had in my head, between myself and the mirror. It was like having a DO NOT DISTURB sign hanging outside the bathroom door. BODY CONFERENCE IN PROGRESS. Please excuse me while I inspect everything that is wrong with me. Privately, I read all the letters in the magazine advice columns to see if someone else's body concerns mirrored my own. Eagerly, I digested the comforting words and practical tips given to "Overweight and Unhappy from Kansas." No one at school let me in on the rules of the game—

Body Image Is All in the Mind

The third essential step to living your life in full and with style takes you on a tour of your body and the feelings you have about it. This is a major learning curve and the exploration will lead you to a wonderful discovery: self-acceptance. On a CBS *48 Hours* segment, "The Price of Perfection" (May 27, 1999), Dan Rather said:

> The number of people who say they are unhappy with the way they look is rising faster than ever. For women, it may be as high as 80 percent. A lot of people who develop illnesses or obsessions about body image say they were relentlessly teased in their youth. Young people especially need to get the message. Self-esteem has to come from inside, not from some trendy standard that few will ever attain. Whatever your age, if you're compromising your health or your happiness, face it. You're paying too high a price for perfection.

The whole subject of the body is what I call the "argument." The argument goes something like this: My body's okay; I'm okay. My body's not okay; I'm not okay. I have had the same argument with my own body. Throughout adolescence, I weighed myself every morning and evening on the scale that was kept in the storage closet at home. As a teenager, I never wanted to talk openly about my body to anyone. Forget it. No, the "argument" could only be had in my head, between myself and the mirror. It was like having a DO NOT DISTURB sign hanging outside the bathroom door. BODY CONFERENCE IN PROGRESS. Please excuse me while I inspect everything that is wrong with me. Privately, I read all the letters in the magazine advice columns to see if someone else's body concerns mirrored my own. Eagerly, I digested the comforting words and practical tips given to "Overweight and Unhappy from Kansas." No one at school let me in on the rules of the game—

that every girl there was having the same argument with her body. I only understood the outcome: the "winners" were thin and the "losers" were fat.

I wanted to disown my body and take off my skin. If only my fat had a zipper. I hoped to leave it at home while I went shopping, put it under my seat while I sat at the movies, dissolve it with soap as I took a shower, and hang it up in the closet before I went to bed. How do you feel about the body in which you spend every waking moment and every night asleep?

"One thing that contributes to the difference among women in the amount of uneasiness they feel about their bodies, several studies show, is how much their parents and friends emphasized their appearance as a child," says Laura Fraser in her book *Losing It: False Hopes and Fat Profits in the Diet Industry* (New York: Penguin, 1998). Camryn Manheim, Susan Moses, Angellika Morton, and I know all too well the truth of Laura's words.

What's left to say about Camryn Manheim? Not only has she received national recognition and respect as the formidable Ellenor in the widely acclaimed *The Practice* but she also stood up for all us "fat girls" as she accepted her first Emmy in 1998 for playing that very role. Voluptuous, daring, outspoken, and gorgeous, Camryn is my shining star. I will continue to share my fashion expertise with her to help her look beautiful, whether she's walking down the red carpet or being photographed for fashion magazines—just as long as she lets me. Camryn has also written an autobiography, which was a *New York Times* best-seller, *"Wake Up, I'm Fat!"* It is based on her one-woman show.

CAMRYN'S STORY

My parents have always been offended by my weight, embarrassed maybe. They had hounded me throughout my childhood about my weight. And they did what any good parent in Southern California would do: they sent me to psychiatrists, to hypnotists; they bribed me. When I was eleven I signed my first contract: "If you lose 15 pounds by March we'll buy you a brand new bike." And I signed it. "If you lose 30 pounds by September we'll buy you an 8-track player." And I signed it. I got the feeling my parents would have sold their souls if it would have made me thin.

Shame arrived right on schedule with the onset of puberty, and I began covering my body at all costs. We lived in Long Beach and the whole time I was there, I remained vigilant about never, ever letting people see my body. I'd wear the heaviest jeans and the baggiest shirts I could find. It was my uniform, my armor. I didn't even want to know I had a body. Because knowing led to crisis: "Oh, my God, I have a body. What am I going to do with it? Oh, shit."

Camryn's recollection is included in her autobiography *"Wake Up, I'm Fat!"* Her book clearly states that her relationship with her parents has come full-circle. Camryn has totally resolved the feelings she once had for her parents. The relationship she shares with them today is one based on complete support and genuine love for each other. Like myself in Step 1, and Camryn in her book, we want you to realize there is hope and a way for everyone who has struggled with their parents to repair and heal the past hurts and old wounds. The point I make with choosing this story of Camryn's is that the seeds of body shame are sown so young.

Susan Moses can well relate. The first time I met her, she exuded such confidence about her body that I felt better just being in the same room with her. Susan has styled many a fashion story for magazines and dressed superstar Brandy for most of her television and movie roles, music videos, and personal appearances for the past five years.

SUSAN'S STORY

I wasn't always comfortable with my body. This, in turn, affected how I felt about myself. At school, I was an A-plus student. No one could put me down in that respect, but you could offend me about my size. I was in the final grade before high school. It was the end of registration and we were about to leave for our first class of the day. I remember some boys at the back of the class throwing scrunched-up paper on my desk and the girls around me talking about the sneakers the girl across from me was wearing. When roll was called, I answered to my name, and a couple of boys started teasing me about my body under the breezy summer clothes I had worn that day. I ignored their icy gibes but felt my cheeks burn with anger and humiliation. When registration ended, I picked up my bag and started to leave the classroom. The teacher was standing at the front of the class, chatting with two of my girlfriends. I overheard her saying to them, "You know, if Susan doesn't lose weight, no one's going to like her when she gets to high school." I guess she hadn't realized that I was still within hearing distance. I walked out, opened my locker, and started to cry into it. To her, my body was unacceptable and so, I thought, was I.

Our feelings about our bodies defy logic and reason. We've all experienced incidents like the one Susan described. As you know, my mother perpetuated the idea that my weight precluded me from being happy. But body image really is all in the mind. Angellika Morton was brought up to feel totally comfortable with her body. Last year, she was chosen to join the Models' Hall of Fame, not only as a woman of color but also as its first plus-size model.

ANGELLIKA'S STORY

Sure, I have "bad days," like everyone else, and I just don't look in the mirror. My Italian mother always went topless at the beach on summer vacations we took as a kid, and consequently, I never owned a whole swimsuit. I didn't really think about it until a few years ago. I was with a friend, working in Miami, and we planned to spend a day at the beach. She and I had similar figures, all curve. We arranged to meet on the beach one blazing summer afternoon, and I had already stripped down to a bright orange thong. Nothing else. My friend found me sitting on a towel, rubbing sunscreen onto my face and arms. She was dressed in an oversized cotton shirt, knee-length shorts, and held a beach bag defensively across her chest. She looked at me strangely. I looked up at her, wondering whether she didn't like what she saw. Still standing, she asked me, "Are you comfortable like that?" I had to pause for a moment to think about her question as she stared at my butt. Although I replied, "Yeah!" and urged her to take off her pants and lie out in her underwear, a part of me questioned whether my body was unacceptable to my friend. I couldn't put on a bikini top. I didn't have one.

Susan Moses can well relate. The first time I met her, she exuded such confidence about her body that I felt better just being in the same room with her. Susan has styled many a fashion story for magazines and dressed superstar Brandy for most of her television and movie roles, music videos, and personal appearances for the past five years.

SUSAN'S STORY

I wasn't always comfortable with my body. This, in turn, affected how I felt about myself. At school, I was an A-plus student. No one could put me down in that respect, but you could offend me about my size. I was in the final grade before high school. It was the end of registration and we were about to leave for our first class of the day. I remember some boys at the back of the class throwing scrunched-up paper on my desk and the girls around me talking about the sneakers the girl across from me was wearing. When roll was called, I answered to my name, and a couple of boys started teasing me about my body under the breezy summer clothes I had worn that day. I ignored their icy gibes but felt my cheeks burn with anger and humiliation. When registration ended, I picked up my bag and started to leave the classroom. The teacher was standing at the front of the class, chatting with two of my girlfriends. I overheard her saying to them, "You know, if Susan doesn't lose weight, no one's going to like her when she gets to high school." I guess she hadn't realized that I was still within hearing distance. I walked out, opened my locker, and started to cry into it. To her, my body was unacceptable and so, I thought, was I.

Our feelings about our bodies defy logic and reason. We've all experienced incidents like the one Susan described. As you know, my mother perpetuated the idea that my weight precluded me from being happy. But body image really is all in the mind. Angellika Morton was brought up to feel totally comfortable with her body. Last year, she was chosen to join the Models' Hall of Fame, not only as a woman of color but also as its first plus-size model.

ANGELLIKA'S STORY

Sure, I have "bad days," like everyone else, and I just don't look in the mirror. My Italian mother always went topless at the beach on summer vacations we took as a kid, and consequently, I never owned a whole swimsuit. I didn't really think about it until a few years ago. I was with a friend, working in Miami, and we planned to spend a day at the beach. She and I had similar figures, all curve. We arranged to meet on the beach one blazing summer afternoon, and I had already stripped down to a bright orange thong. Nothing else. My friend found me sitting on a towel, rubbing sunscreen onto my face and arms. She was dressed in an oversized cotton shirt, knee-length shorts, and held a beach bag defensively across her chest. She looked at me strangely. I looked up at her, wondering whether she didn't like what she saw. Still standing, she asked me, "Are you comfortable like that?" I had to pause for a moment to think about her question as she stared at my butt. Although I replied, "Yeah!" and urged her to take off her pants and lie out in her underwear, a part of me questioned whether my body was unacceptable to my friend. I couldn't put on a bikini top. I didn't have one.

The feelings of inadequacy that I've had about my body came from a result of someone else projecting the fears and insecurities they had onto me. My time in the theater was fraught with body issues, and I wasn't given the roles I wanted on account of my size. But I was uncomfortable with my body long before I even got to college.

MY STORY

Adolescence was very hard for me because I was considered "big." I wore a size thirteen in the world of "Juniorland," and most of the girls wore a size five or seven. Every Saturday afternoon, my friends and I went to the mall. The first thing we'd do was go and buy an Orange Julius, a creamy fruit shake with more calories than I could count. I decided I couldn't order one. You see, at twelve, six months after seeing the psychologist, I was already on my first diet. I'd say that I needed to use the rest room and instead sneak over to another Orange Julius counter and drink one really quickly. I felt so ashamed at having to drink it in secret.

After drinks, we'd go to Marianne's, Michigan's version of Express or Strawberry. It was the time of shirts tucked in and shrunken tops. And my friends would all try on clothes that I couldn't wear. I'd pick up something in the biggest size, go into the dressing room, look in the mirror, and feel too embarrassed to go back out. I would peer through the side of the curtain, and I saw how the clothes looked on Sheryl and Debbie. Those clothes never looked like that on me. But I really wanted those clothes. I'd make sure the curtain was closed again, stand and face the dressing room, and say, "Why can't I fit in? Why can't I fit into this? Why can't I fit into the group? Why don't they understand who I am?"

It was a lonely time for me in my teens. I had to go around with the girls in the pack, who treated me like an outsider. I didn't vocalize my interest in boys. And I couldn't wear what they wore. They didn't really have anything to say to me. I could be their friend. But that didn't mean I could be their "girlfriend." And I wanted so desperately to be their girlfriend. I believed the only way I could was if my body looked like theirs. Changing my clothes twenty times before school, I felt that nothing looked good on me because I never looked like those girls in those clothes. I'd get so frustrated because I felt there was something wrong with me. The sole reason for this? My body wasn't like theirs.

Whenever I'd feel hurt and upset, I'd escape to the "island." It was a cluster of trees in the middle of the street that formed an island. I'd take the dog and my suitcase and leave home. I just felt alone. I spent my time on the island reading. I knew Betsy's, Tacy's, and Tibb's whole lives and *Charlotte's Web* inside out. They became my friends. As I read their stories, I felt they understood my anguish over not being picked for a game, getting my period later than the other girls in my grade, and the fact that neither Craig nor Kevin wanted to kiss me when we played Spin the Bottle. I felt much closer to the girls on the page than I did to the girls at the mall.

Now it's time to police your negative body thoughts.

➤ TUNE IN

In your Learning Curves journal, write down your negative body thoughts. Make a list under these two headings: (1) General body thoughts and (2) Specific body part thoughts. Do you have a tendency to use phrases like "my big fat butt" or "thunder thighs"? "My stomach's huge" or "my arms are flabby"? Take these phrases, which you repeat to others and say to yourself, and put them down on paper.

➤ LIVE OUT LOUD

Cinder Ernst, a size-fourteen aerobics teacher for plus-size women and a personal trainer at the World Gym in San Francisco, stresses the importance of becoming your own "negative body thought police." She has seen many women at the gym speaking badly about their own bodies. Cinder has developed a technique that I always use to police my own negative body thoughts.

take these steps:

1. Identify the body part you speak ill of.
2. Go to a mirror and touch that body part.
3. Apologize to the body part you are speaking so negatively about.
4. Repeat the same process with each body part.

As Cinder says, "You need to apologize to those thighs and put your hand on that body part and embrace it. What would you say of someone who was criticizing the way your child or your friend looks? Think how you would feel, and then take those feelings of respect, loyalty, and love a step deeper by defending yourself from a place of loving all of you."

CHANGING THE PACKAGING DOES NOT CHANGE WHO YOU ARE

For years, I tried to make myself something that I wasn't. Why did I want to change my body? I believed that being thin would make me happy. And I certainly wasn't alone in this belief. There are over 30 million women in America on a diet on any given day. I bought into the notion that many women still believe—and perhaps you still do—that the size of my body was my fault. Consequently, I paid most of my salary to a dieting industry that makes from $34 to $50 billion a year (that's about the gross national product of Ireland) from our collective insecurities (John LaRosa, diet industry analyst at Marketdata Research). I've learned through experience, as I hope you will as you read our stories, that neither the "thin equals happy" nor the "being fat is my fault" sentiment is true.

The misconception that our bodies are shaped only by our choices and have little to do with our genes, environment, or even our destinies has created a society that's consumed by chronic dieting and eating disorders. Most interesting are the results of a Gallup poll published in August 1999: "When It Comes to Weight, Americans Are Loosening Their Belts: As Americans Grow Heavier, Satisfaction with Own Weight Remains Steady." Christa Ehmann's research found that "the percentage [of Americans] describing themselves as 'overweight' has dropped, from 48% in 1990 to 39% today."

The media emphasizes the health risks of being overweight as the justification for the continual coverage of dieting. Little attention is given to the adverse effects of losing and regaining weight. A study in the *New England Journal of Medicine* states that the health risks of gaining and losing weight are greater than the health risks of being big.

Being in the magazine business, I also get to read some very interesting studies that most marketers want to keep away from your eyes. *One woman out of every four reports feelings of inadequacy and low self-esteem after reading a fashion magazine for thin-sized women for three minutes.* Remember, most magazines want you to feel that way so that you go out and buy whatever's featured to help you overcome those feelings. The trouble is, the false promise keeps you buying all the latest "miracle products." But your feelings stay the same.

At the root of our desire to change ourselves is the basic feeling that we're lacking in some way. Here's how Susan, Camryn, Angellika, and I have tried to change our bodies in order to find happiness.

SUSAN'S STORY

As a teenager, I made the choice to change my body. I starved it. After a rough ride weightwise through high school, at eighteen I was anorexic. I had just split up with my first serious boyfriend, whose parting words before leaving me for a smaller girl were, "I think you're really pretty, but I wish you'd just lose a few pounds." Just a few pounds, huh? Well, eighty-five pounds later, throwing up food as if it were a contaminated substance, I was skinny and sick. School ended and I was home for the holiday vacation. The clothes were hanging off me and yet I still felt big. My goal was to lose twenty pounds more. Then I'd be happy. On my way home one night, waiting for the D train at 161st Street by

Yankee Stadium, too weak to stand, I fell on the track. A guy rushed down to pick me up, and I was covered in bruises. The train arrived soon after and the man helped me to my seat. I felt sore and embarrassed. Finally, I made it home, where, ironically, my mother had just returned from a funeral. She was horrified at the state I was in. My brother greeted me by calling me "Texas" because my left cheek looked like the map of that southern state. My family immediately took me to the doctor, and thankfully, I had done no major damage to myself except that I needed to have my eyebrow stitched up.

The incident was my wake-up call. Starving myself in a desperate effort to change my body didn't make me happy. I had gone to great lengths in order to change my body and all I felt was more depressed and unworthy. I believed that I would look better one day. That "one day" never came and the journey home almost became my last.

The "make them like me" potion is not found by starvation or drugs. But Camryn tried it. And sadly, yes, it was almost at the cost of her life.

CAMRYN'S STORY

During my three years at NYU I had developed elaborate defense mechanisms and an ordered system of self-reliance. Much of this, of course, was a facade. I was honing my lying skills as I perfected my acting skills. I was putting forth the image of the jolly fat girl to cover up a morass of self-hatred, despair and deceit. I always thought that if I were thin, men would be attracted to me and that would make everything all right. But it doesn't matter if *they* like you if you hate yourself. I was told and believed that it was my fault for being fat and if I wanted to change it I could. Not only did I suffer the slings and arrows of being a fat girl in this society, but I suffered the shame and humiliation of knowing it was all at my hand, and that is why I built up the armor and the weapons to keep anyone from discovering it. But the system was built on a precarious foundation; lies and amphetamines do not a sturdy base make.

I had cut myself off from everybody who cared about me. I only wanted to be with people who didn't care about me because they wouldn't challenge me. So there I was, at some guy's house, doing speed [the guaranteed weight-loss method of the moment] and philosophizing about anything at all as long as we didn't have to talk about ourselves, when my chest began to tighten. I was short of breath. I lost my bearings. Waves of fear and paranoia swept over me. I thought I was dying. I sat on his bathroom floor until morning and realized that my heart couldn't take any more. In every sense. After that near-fatal overdose, I had two choices. I could continue down this path of self-destruction or I could grow up.

When Angellika chose to change her body for a bigger one, due to a medical condition, she was faced with deciding what she really wanted from life. What she didn't expect was how quickly she would make her decision.

ANGELLIKA'S STORY

At twenty-one, I had just received my child psychology degree and felt good about myself. But I chose to give up my size-eight figure after being told that I had a fibroid tumor the size of a grapefruit. It's a condition that some of the women on my mother's side of the family have had. It's not life-threatening, and I didn't have to have the tumor removed. No treatment would mean, however, that I would never be able to have children. And I really wanted children.

I met with my doctor, who explained gravely what the treatment would involve. "I have to tell you," he said, "that the hormone, Lupron, has side effects, one of which is gaining weight." It sounded as if he was consoling me and warning me of the consequences. I asked him, "Is that the worst thing that can happen to me?" He didn't reply, but he left me alone in his office for a few minutes. I asked myself, How would I feel if I really gained weight? Fine, was my answer. I consented to the treatment and was given the hormone. In eight months, I gained a total of fifteen pounds. I honestly felt sexier and more womanly than ever. The doctors were able to remove the tumor successfully. After the operation, I stayed at a heavier weight and have remained at that weight to this day.

What shocked me more than anything was the doctor's attitude that day in his office. Changing my body for a bigger one made absolutely no difference to the fundamentally happy way I felt about myself. What did make a difference to me was the possibility of having a family.

When it came to my body, I had to repeat a learning curve. Although I had firmly stood up for myself and my body to the college professor who wrote me that note I mentioned in Step 1, five years later I chose to fall into the hands of a diet doctor.

MY STORY

While temping at the American fashion house of Perry Ellis, I sat at my desk during lunch one day and read the latest issue of *New Woman* magazine. On page 48, two pictures appeared of the same woman in a leotard, before and after dieting. The headline read something like this: DIETING CAN CHANGE YOUR LIFE! She had lost forty-seven pounds. It sounded great. I was twenty-five, in a job I was limited by, and in a body for which I had to have my clothes altered. I was still angry at myself that I couldn't conform. I couldn't wear the regulation uniform at Perry Ellis. I was miserable. So, I thought, If I could change, my whole life would change. I'd get the boy, have a life, have the career, and I could wear the clothes. Losing weight, I was convinced, was the key that would unlock Pandora's box.

The article provided the name of the "Miracle Man" who had changed this woman's body, a body shape similar to my own. I looked up his number in the Yellow Pages and called immediately for an appointment. I saw this diet doctor the next day. I walked into his Upper East Side office with a copy of the article in my hand, wanting him to do the same as he had done for the woman in the article. Boy, was he handsome. Richard Gere–like. So gorgeous that I would have done anything for him. And I did.

He put me on a diet of powders for breakfast, lunch, and dinner. That's all I ate, if you can call that eating, for ten months. The small box of diet cookies he said I could "treat" myself to once a day were all gone by the time I returned to work after leaving his office. It was the best lunch of the week. Besides seeing the diet doctor, whose weekly visits I looked forward to, I had to see the nutritionist, the nurse, and the psychologist. I saw everybody. The first question they'd ask me was, "How was your week?" My answer depended on how much weight I'd lost. Usually, I answered, "It's been a hell of a week," for no reason other than I hadn't lost enough weight. There would be some weeks when I wouldn't go because I didn't think I'd lost sufficient weight to please the handsome doctor. So I'd skip eating the powders in order to lose more weight and then I'd go and pay them all a visit, and I'd smile at the diet doctor, who told me I was "doing very well."

It was ten months of misery. Still, I didn't feel attractive enough. But there was a part of me that thought that the diet doctor would like me if I was thinner. After ten months, I returned to the doctor's office and he weighed me. I had lost seventy-five pounds—twenty-eight pounds more than the woman in the article. I was considered a total diet success story. Break out the champagne and give me an honorary membership.

Despite the "success," I wasn't happy. Losing weight did not "change my life." The only thing I was was smaller. I still had the same job, wasn't dating, and the diet doctor didn't like me any better at a smaller size. Nothing changed. I could not believe that I had trusted someone other than myself to tell me if I was okay or not. I had let a diet doctor tell me what it would take for me to feel better. What I should have done was to explore why I believed I wasn't okay, before allowing someone to tell me that I'd be happy if I lost weight. I vowed to myself that this time I had learned the lesson.

It's time for you to tune in.

This visualization was developed by Jane R. Hirschmann and Carol H. Munter in their best-selling book *When Women Stop Hating Their Bodies: Freeing Yourself from Food and Weight Obsession* (New York: Fawcett, 1995).

Read the following passage several times, as I did, lie down on your bed or sofa, and write your answers down in your journal.

Suspend your disbelief for the moment and imagine that the atmosphere is about to be infused with a strange and powerful substance—a substance that will make it impossible for anyone to ever gain or lose another pound. Your body and the bodies of everyone you know will remain exactly at their current weight.

How would you lead your life in this new atmosphere? What would you wear once you are no longer waiting to change size? Would you take that trip to the beach you have been postponing until you lose weight? And how about the exercise regime you are planning to begin? Are you still interested, even though you know it will not have any impact on your size?

Before you answer these questions, consider this one final piece of information. This strange and powerful substance that you are now inhaling with every breath has an additional quality: It creates an environment in which no one's body is considered more beautiful than any other, an environment in which bad body thoughts no longer exist, in your mind, or in anyone else's, and all bodies are regarded as lovely and interesting.

How would you feel living in a world in which the size and shape of your body were regarded without any judgment? How would you feel walking down the street, sitting on a bus, buying your groceries, and eating your lunch in a world in which you knew that your body's size and shape were just fine?

Right now, such a world is only a fantasy. Regardless of what is happening in the world around you, however, you can create the kind of acceptance we are talking about, *within yourself.* You can create a world in which you see your body *as it is* and enjoy it. You can challenge all the ideas you have unconsciously internalized about how bodies should look. You can take your bad body thoughts and put them aside. You can dress yourself in ways that please you. And you can begin to live the kind of life you have put on hold "until I lose weight."

The authors of *When Women Stop Hating Their Bodies* note at the end of the above visualization exercise, "The power to create an environment of self-acceptance is within you."

➤ LIVE OUT LOUD

In your Learning Curves journal, list all the things that you don't do, or didn't do in the past, because of your weight and your body. List everything—try to remember as many experiences as possible. Here are a few ideas to get you started.

Go to the beach.

Make love with the lights on.

Wear a short skirt.

Speak to a group.

Go to the gym.

Smile at a stranger.

Ask for a raise.

You can see how much you are allowing yourself to miss because of your thinking, "When I lose weight, then I can do that." It's time to step out from behind your fear and do something that you have always wanted to do. Choose the one thing on your list that you would like to do more than the others. This is *the* week to do it.

I often used to think to myself, "If and when I do this, then I will be able to do

➤ TUNE IN

that." For example, "I'm not going to buy this until I lose weight." Or, "I'm not going to join the gym until I feel comfortable enough to go." If I hadn't rejoined the gym when I said I would, I would not be ready or feel comfortable enough to do the 5K walk through New York's Central Park for the cure for cancer every spring. Ask yourself, "How can I help myself today?" Who cares about when? It's now that's important. Your body lives with you this minute. This is your skin. Thinking that you're going to be more perfect tomorrow or next month is not really honoring what you've been given today.

I am not here to tell you that you can't change your body. But I do want you to think about your choices and the effects your decisions will have on you: physical, emotional, and financial. Consider dropping the "argument."

LEARNING CURVE 10

LOVING YOURSELF REQUIRES LOVING ALL OF YOU

After having the negative effects of yo-yo dieting confirmed for me by seeing a series of nutritionists, and having counted the mental price—depression and self-loathing—I paid for all the diets, I finally began to drop the "argument."

The road to self-acceptance hasn't been easy, and there are still days when I feel that my stomach could be a little bit firmer. But the reality is that those days happen so rarely. It's taken me years to accept all of me, even though my fleshy upper arms have also caused me plenty of grief over the years, but the reward is well worth it. By learning to accept your body, you haven't opted for a round-trip to the land of "grin and bear it." You, my friend, have chosen a one-way ticket to freedom.

Self-acceptance, as any dictionary will tell you, is all about "providing an affirmative response and approving of your own identity." For me now, my body is something that I realize I own, need to take care of, and truly get comfortable with, if I am to live my life in full.

You know that my mother taught me that happiness came in a very specific package. One that I didn't fit into, and, I have also learned, neither do most women in the world. Let me give you a few vital statistics from a television special called *Life in the Fat Lane* (which aired in 1995).

> Height of the average American woman: 5′4″
>
> Height of the average female model: 5′9″
>
> Weight of the average American woman in pounds: 144–150
>
> Weight of the average female model: 123

I know through working in fashion that there are eight supermodels and 8 billion regular women in the world. In 1997, the Body Shop built an advertising campaign on this premise. I don't want to burst a bubble, but you and I are never going to look like Cindy Crawford. Sorry. But I can also tell you that there are not merely eight beautiful women in the world. Realize that there is one supermodel in your life. That, my friend, is you. Read how my friends and I learned how to live in our skins.

SUSAN'S STORY

It took me two years to recover fully from anorexia. In that time, I realized that it wasn't food I'd spent my life fighting; it was me. After the incident on the train track, my mother bought me a gratitude journal. Every day, I wrote how lucky I was to be alive. I saw a therapist for a while and my mother reinforced all the good qualities I had. And I prayed. I had always prayed, even in my darkest moments. Though I never felt alone back then, I was so angry at God for making me the fat one in the family. But when I went for my spiritual food in church every Sunday, I began to accept me. All of me. Not just the brain and the ambition but my body, as well. The body that I now wanted to live in. Wanted to love. I filled every page in my journal, describing not just how happy I felt to be alive but how happy I was to be me. I'd never felt happy before.

I thank God that I got away from the guy who told me to lose weight. And I realize that if I hadn't accepted all of me, every part I love and every part I don't, I would not be happy today. I would not have created the opening to allow Craig into my life, the husband I married last July. I wouldn't be able to do my job as a stylist had I not learned to get comfortable with my own body. I can honestly say that I wouldn't change a thing. I realize that no one has the right to tell anyone they're not okay. That is, unless you allow them to. I'll never do that again.

As Angellika discovered, not everyone's as happy as she is about her own body.

ANGELLIKA'S STORY

The first thing I see when I look in the mirror are my child-bearing hips. I love my curves and I want them to stay there. But some people, women in particular, find the way I feel about my body quite intimidating. Not many women, even thin women, are comfortable with their own bodies. I recently went to my best friend's wedding on the sun-kissed island of Jamaica in tropical October, where the humidity was at a record high. I spent four days in a hotel with the rest of the wedding party. On the first night, I was introduced to a couple, and we all seemed to hit it off. But things began to take a turn. By the second night, after I'd spent a day at the beach and dined with them, the girlfriend, petite and pretty, started making nasty remarks. I sensed hostility. We had all joined the wedding party on an evening cruise and I could see the hotel lights on the island lit behind me. I felt really sexy and good about myself. I was happy. The couple greeted me on the deck and the boyfriend said, "You look really beautiful in red." The temperature between his girlfriend and me suddenly dropped.

He went off to fetch the cocktails and she and I stood alone. She looked at me with what I can only describe as an envious glance, and, annoyed, announced, "I don't want you walking around dressed like that. You know my boyfriend likes you." I was wearing a sundress, not a thong bikini. She then added scathingly, "You're a *plus*-size model, aren't you?" All eyes were on us. After a short pause, I said to her, "Your boyfriend just likes what he sees." She thought that if she exposed my career, the guests would find me less beautiful. It totally backfired. As she walked away, the other guests approached me with great interest about me and my work. She didn't speak to me for the rest of the wedding. I realized that the confidence I have about *my* body isn't always met with welcome, because others haven't found the confidence within themselves. They think, What's she got that I haven't? The answer is that I live in my skin and I want to stay there.

In her book, Camryn states that her fat—her friend—is male. She adds: "I know it says something about me that I consider the personification of my fat to be male, but over the years, I've realized that its tyranny is quintessentially masculine. Which isn't to say that I blame men for my fat. No, rather I just view my fat as Mussolini. It is a terrible oppressor that makes the shame run on time."

CAMRYN'S STORY

It was during *"Wake Up, I'm Fat!"* that I started to figure out the relationship I had with my fat. What if I stopped blaming him for everything? What if I stopped using him as an excuse? What if I stopped hiding behind him and entered into a covenant with myself that if I failed as an actor or a lover, it was my fault, my responsibility? It wouldn't be easy. I would have so much more at stake, which meant I was going to have to work harder, prepare more thoroughly, and redouble my commitment to my art. From that point forward, I wouldn't let myself off the hook so easily with a simple "They didn't choose me because I was fat." No, if they didn't choose me, it was because I didn't wow them. I stopped relying on my ever-present alibi and put all my energies into wowing them. These were my first baby steps on the journey of self-acceptance. And a funny thing happened on the way to the self-love forum: I learned that confidence, courage, and a little bit of sass can be very seductive. We've reached a peaceful harmony, me and my fat. I can't say that on some days I don't get a little twinge of self-loathing but, for the most part, me and my fat are getting along fine. I'm still a misfit. Only now I'm proud not to fit in.

Like Camryn, I'm also proud not to fit in. These days when people ask me what my size is, I say to them, "*My* size." Confused, some press further: "So, what size is that?" I reply, "The *right* size, for *me*." I learned this lesson on the designer floor at Bloomingdale's.

MY STORY

My Perry Ellis days had ended, I'd powdered myself out, and my weight had crept back up to its natural size. I had found my comfort zone as a size sixteen. I could go into any department store and try on clothes. After a time working in a plus-size specialty retail store called Ashanti, I began to get a sense of how important it is to feel good in your clothes. I was helping women figure out what they wanted to say about themselves. But what did I want my body to say about me? One day, I saw a new Donna Karan dress on the designer floor in Bloomingdale's. She called it her "Catwoman" dress. It looked like something a superhuman would wear. It was a deep, plunging V-necked long-sleeved black wool jersey evening dress with a fish tail. Many nights, at around 7:00 P.M., I'd go to visit this dress. Shivers went down my spine every time I saw it. After the fifth consecutive night of going to the department store and looking at this dress, I finally ventured into the Donna Karan boutique. I tried on a number of other outfits, but my eyes were fixated on the silent mannequin wearing that dress. I plucked up the courage to ask to try on the dress and I took it into the dressing room. Standing in my bare feet, I nervously slipped the dress onto my body. The three-way mirror told me something I never knew before: the truth. Not only was this a fabulous dress but it also looked fabulous on me.

I left the dressing room and started sauntering around other boutiques on the floor—into Calvin Klein, through Bill Blass, across Chanel, and around Oscar de la Renta. Remember, this was *the* floor! I felt six feet tall and drop-dead gorgeous. I felt as if I were in the Miss America pageant.

I realized that I had the power to feel feminine and sexy. When I returned to the Donna Karan boutique, the sales associate said to me, "Do you know that every single man has turned around to look at you?" I honestly hadn't noticed. Feeling great, I went back into the dressing room. I was in there for a long time. Taking several deep breaths, I realized that I had just had the experience of knowing what it was like to be in my body. For me, it was the closest I would get to walking around nude in public. There was not a curve this dress didn't accentuate. It made me completely aware of my size. And you know what? My size wasn't so bad. It actually made me look great in the dress. I had finally done something that I had never done. That was, to own my body. I wanted to laugh and cry both at the same time. I looked at myself in the mirror one more time before taking off this twelve-hundred-dollar dress. I never bought the dress. It was much more than I could afford. But I couldn't put any price tag on the lesson I learned that Thursday night. And I left Bloomingdale's a very happy woman.

Today, I ask you to love your body. Begin by taking a look.

➤ TUNE IN

First, create a safe space, somewhere that feels friendly. Find a full-length mirror in your home and close the door. This is the toughest exercise I will ask you to do, but I feel we know each other well enough for me to make this request. Take off your clothes and look at yourself naked in the mirror. If this seems too scary right now, just stand in front of the mirror fully dressed but without your shoes. It's more important that you do the exercise than not. Really see what you have. Observe every curve. What do you see? Okay, you can put your clothes back on now. Body conference over.

> In your Learning Curves journal, write down a list of everything you love about your body. On a separate list, write down every part you find hard to embrace. What are your complaints? "My breasts are too big; my stomach's not flat; my feet are ugly." Make your list. Now comes the hard part. For every part of your body that you listed as a problem area, I'd like you to write a positive reason to love that part. "I love my _____ because _____ " So, for example, if you find it hard to embrace your stomach because it's not flat, remember that your children lived there before they were born. Maybe your nose is a certain shape because you take after the father you adore. This is what I wrote about the hard parts to embrace in my journal.
>
> *I love my stomach because I have the softest skin and my boyfriends love to rest their heads on it.*
>
> *I love my breasts because I can wear really low-cut dresses without a bra.*
>
> *I love my curly hair because it's sexy and men love to run their fingers through the curls.*

I want you to write a sentence on why you love every part of yourself. It may take a while to think of a positive reason for everything. Take your time. Go back to the mirror and back to the journal. But start today. Meditate on it. Think about why your body is the way it is.

When your list is complete, you will see that there is a reason for you to love each and every part of yourself.

➤ LIVE OUT LOUD

Go back to the mirror and do this exercise once a week.

1. Undress and look at your body.
2. Focus on the areas that you are having the most difficulties accepting.
3. Look at each area and say aloud why you love that part of yourself.
4. If you feel resistance, gently affirm your body mantra.
5. Don't be angry if you don't love your whole body overnight. This may take weeks or even months.
6. Repeat this process until you feel a level of comfort with your whole body.

Your body will thank you for being allowed to be just fine the way it is and your brain will thank you for ending the complaints. Living in your skin is about you appreciating what you love about your body and embracing the parts you don't. No one says it's easy. If we could exchange one forehead for another, one set of legs for another, and one pair of feet for another, we'd all be walking around in extreme physical pain and look like the extras in *Star Wars*. Now when I look in the mirror, my stomach is the first thing I touch. And embracing my upper arms allows me to give someone else, a man across from me at a dinner table, for example, the permission to touch me there without my thinking, Oh my God! That's probably why I wear so many sleeveless tops. Remember, my wish is that this book reveals to you your uniqueness. Your individual style. You have the body given to *you*. If you don't learn to get comfortable with it, who can?

TLC: A Little Bit of Love Goes a Long Way

Living in your skin doesn't end at acceptance. It's only the beginning. Your body, like a relative you admire, needs to be treated with respect. Yes, even your body has feelings. Neglect it and your body feels ignored. Respect it with all the appreciation you can give it and your body will respond by making you look and feel better. Remember, a little bit of love goes a long way.

How do you show your body the respect it truly deserves? The answer is to give it TLC—tender loving care. I'm not suggesting extravagant or expensive gestures of love. But, hey, if you want to, your body's not going to fight you on that. Remember, your body is your friend. And like all true friendships, it's what you give that counts.

This is one of my favorite subjects and I want to share it with you. The way we treat our bodies is so important for our self-esteem. You've acknowledged the parts you love and the parts you are now beginning to embrace. And yet we haven't always been kind to our bodies, have we? I've punished my body for looking the way it has looked. I hadn't taken it for a walk in a long time, I wouldn't treat it to a new lipstick. I rarely had a massage. At some time or another, we've denied our bodies their purpose. That is, to enjoy every experience we have with ourselves. We've put our bodies through grueling tests of endurance to see if they'd crack under the strain. Our bodies are still here, still with us. Still our friend.

SUSAN'S STORY

Before I'd fully accepted the body I have, I wasn't kind to my body. As you know, there was a part of me that wanted to make it invisible. I didn't want to show it the world. And, as a result, I didn't care for it. I didn't care whether it looked good or bad, lived or died. I'd spent my money on diet pills, not beauty products. When I was trying to get back on my feet, my cousin gave me a gift. It was for a facial. I'd never had one before. She explained what it was, and I was particularly drawn to the idea of spending time on myself. I scheduled an appointment and spent one of the happiest hours of my life having my face cleansed, toned, and moisturized. I felt so relaxed and so much better about myself.

I've treated my body with respect ever since. Now, at thirty-four years old, I'm a regular at the Mario Badescu Salon in New York for a monthly facial, I give myself eight hours sleep a night, and I exercise and meditate every morning. I feel that as important as it is to feel good about myself on the inside, it's equally important to take care of myself on the outside. Every time I treat myself, no matter how big or how small, I feel like I'm worth every dime. I'm now pretty good to the old girl!

ANGELLIKA'S STORY

The way I treat my body hasn't changed since I was a teenager. I wash my face and body with whatever bar of soap I have, and I rub Vaseline onto my face every night before bed. My mother said that the routine would keep me looking beautiful. And I believe it has. Today, as a thirty-one-year-old woman, there are three things I call "the priority." They are my hands, my feet, and my teeth. Those three parts are the things people notice first. I make sure I see the dentist and have manicures and pedicures on a regular basis. Occasionally, I'll treat myself to a massage because it's the only time no one can reach me by pager, and I think it's important to do something that helps you deal with the stress of life. But the biggest TLC I give myself doesn't come out of a bottle. Every morning, I write in my gratitude journal about whatever good things happened to me the day before. I feel that appreciating my life is the best thing I can do for myself. If I feel good, my body feels good. It's as simple as that.

MY STORY

Even though I work in the fashion and beauty industry, don't think I'm sent invitations for free haircuts or facials many times each week. Often, I go into the drugstore nearest my home and buy the samples. Yes, for ninety-nine cents, I, too, can try whatever's new. I travel with these samples so that I'm not left in a foreign country, leafing through a phrase book to find the Spanish line for "No frizz, eco-friendly, permanent-hold hair gel, please." It just doesn't happen. I love pampering myself. My favorite treats are having my feet rubbed in a reflexology massage and having an herbal wrap—being wrapped in warm, scented towels in a quiet room that plays heavenly New Age music. I pay attention to things that give me pleasure, even small things. For example, when it comes to soaking in my bath, I light candles and burn incense in the bathroom and fill the tub with aromatherapy oils. I look after my hands because, as a child, I loved seeing my mother's and aunt's manicured hands. I've added pedicures to my beauty regimen because painted toes make me feel feminine. I never underestimate the power of a red toe in an open-toed sandal! When I find myself broke at the end of a month and I have to cancel a facial appointment, I mash up an avocado, slice a cucumber to put over my eyes, comb Hellmann's mayonnaise or raw egg through my hair, and sit with the contents of my fridge on my face while I listen to some classical music. You know what it is above all else? I just like being a woman.

Remember, it's important to give yourself TLC, because most of the time you're the only person who'll take care of you. Realize that what you put onto your body is not necessarily about improving or significantly changing your outer appearance. What you are doing is fundamentally acknowledging the respect you have for the body you own.

Tune in to what makes you feel good.

➤ TUNE IN

What have you done for yourself that makes you feel good? Check off the list on next page in the appropriate columns.

	HAVE TRIED	WOULD LIKE TO TRY	WOULD DO REGULARLY
Long, scented bath			
Herbal wrap, seaweed or body-salt scrub			
Manicure at home			
Professional manicure			
Pedicure at home			
Professional pedicure			
Wax paraffin treatment for your hands or feet			
Facial at home			
Professional facial			
Waxing at home			
Professional waxing			
Eyebrow shaping at home			
Professional eyebrow shaping			
Massage			
Go to a day spa			
Spa weekend with a friend			
Regular haircut			
Light candles			
Burn incense			
Keep a gratitude journal			
Pray			

Now that you've checked off the things you love to do for yourself, I'd like you to choose three things you'd like to do for yourself but feel you never would spend the time or money on. You may, if you wish, refer to the above list. Think about every possibility. If you could wave a wand, what would you do for yourself?

➤ LIVE OUT LOUD

Starting today, I'd like you to set aside sixty minutes of personal time each week. Begin a beauty routine at home, such as setting aside an evening to have a long bath, do a face mask, and paint your fingers and toes. Write the time down in your daily planner. Or make an appointment to go to a day spa for a massage or facial, or to have your nails done professionally. Ask friends for recommendations, and, like me, begin to save articles on new spas and salons in your city that the magazines have tried, tested, and rated. Whatever you choose, keep that time for yourself. Acknowledge your body's worth and appreciate everything it does for you.

Remember, your body doesn't have to be a source of pain and you don't have to be something that you're not. "Being thin doesn't always guarantee satisfaction. Nor does being fat always result in poor self-image. As with compulsive dieting, it isn't the size of a person that matters so much as the weight of her discontent," says Laura Fraser, author of *Losing It: False Hopes and Fat Profits in the Diet Industry.* Your body is with you to be your friend and help you to experience the pleasures of life. If we could forgive ourselves for all that we've done to our bodies, we'd be writing a letter on paper the size of the Great Wall of China. Realize that you are perfect the way you are. Accept that your body is a positive reflection of yourself. And above all, treat it well; treat it with respect. Give it love. It lives with you now, this moment as you read this book. Be proud of the body you have. It's the part of you that you'll spend your whole life with.

Mind over Matter

To begin a healthy relationship with your food, you must learn to be aware of what you eat and what your body needs. Take time to savor and create a sense of yourself bite by bite. Finding out what you like is the key to finding out what you're like.

MOLLY O'NEILL, *NEW YORK TIMES* FOOD CRITIC

Awareness Is the Key to Understanding Your Relationship with Food

I was considering making this Learning Curve 13 because the number thirteen has always been considered unlucky. I actually consider it lucky. If you look at a baker's dozen, I get one extra. But no matter how hard I tried, this learning curve was the twelfth stop on the journey. The subjects of food and exercise are the most difficult for full-figured women because these are the two areas that are considered our Achilles' heel. As the assumption goes, we eat too much and exercise too little. Sound familiar? But we are not alone on this learning curve. Journalist Martha McCully has said, ". . . like so many other women in their teens, 20's, 30's, 40's (not our entire lives, I hope), my relationship with food is complex. It is part psychological, part schizophrenic, part symptomatic of some anxiety I'll never understand" (*New York Times,* August 1, 1999).

I've tried the suggested diet programs—Dr. Atkins's, powders, the Diet Center's, and even the infamous Hollywood grapefruit diet—stepped, treadmilled, and spun in many a gym, only to find that there were better ways *for me* to eat and work out. There are so many theories: *the* right way to eat and *the* right exercise plan. I don't have the "right" answers to solving these theories. But I have learned that living your life in full requires a change in your attitude to food and exercise.

"A new movement is rising from the turmoil of widespread frustration with diets that don't work, pressures to be thin, and the crises in eating disorders that grip America. It calls for wellness, not weight loss, and it focuses on the three following factors: (1) feeling good about oneself; (2) eating well in a natural, relaxed way; and (3) being comfortably active," wrote editor Frances M. Berg in the September/October 1992 issue of *Healthy Weight Journal.*

Let's begin with food. We label all sorts of things "good" and "bad," including ourselves. We label the food good or bad, eat the food, and judge ourselves accordingly. I can tell you that a chocolate muffin never made anyone a "bad" person. And does eating a mixed green salad make you a "good" one? Logically, no. Emotionally, yes.

"Very few American women I know are like some Italian friends of mine, who take passionate interest in what they cook and eat. They drizzle olive oil on vegetables, relish every bite of their meals, and eat dessert or not, as they please. Eating, for them, is a sensual experience, not a fearful one. They never feel guilty afterward. Food isn't 'good' or 'bad' depending on the calories or fat grams it contains, but according to how fresh it is, and how lovingly prepared. My Italian friends don't binge when they're upset because food doesn't have the power to overwhelm or hurt them," writes Laura Fraser in *Losing It.*

All the great memories, the celebrations, and the occasions in which food has played an integral part have become clouded with the "cans" and "cannots" that surround us. I'd like you to explore the relationship you have with food so that we move beyond the idea that food is somehow connected to your self-esteem. Because it isn't. But the stories illustrate that food is often connected to feelings of guilt and shame.

Wendy Shanker is a stand-up comedian, performing her one-woman shows on New York's comedy circuit. She is also a writer and contributes to magazines such as *Mode, Bust,* and *Hues.* Wendy is as comfortable talking about female body hair as she is about the characters on *Frasier.* She has written for ABC, Lifetime, MTV, and VH1. Now she's breathing life into the new women's television network, Oxygen.

WENDY'S STORY

My family and I went out for a meal the evening before my umpteenth rejoin of Optifast. We all sat around a big round table and the waiter handed out the menus. Conversation paused for a moment for us to glance at the list. I read the whole menu and the only thing that sounded appealing to me was a Caesar salad. When the waiter returned to the table and took down our orders, I asked for the Caesar salad. Halfway through the meal, my father abruptly interrupted the conversation, put down his knife and fork, and looked at me. He yelled, "How can you sit here looking the way you do and eat that fattening salad?" The whole restaurant fell into silence. I just sat there shocked and embarrassed. Then I started to cry. I excused myself from the table and bolted out of the restaurant. While the rest of my family finished their meal, I kept asking myself, "Aren't I allowed to have one last moment of pleasure, since I'm going to do this crazy diet for them?" Something in my head said that Caesar salad was okay, but for everybody else in my family, it wasn't. Maybe I was wrong.

My meeting with Molly O'Neill was coincidental. She was interviewing Camryn for a magazine article in a designer's showroom when I was there helping Camryn choose a dress to wear to the Golden Globe Awards. Molly *loves* food. I read her food page every Sunday in the *New York Times.* Molly writes about the art and celebration of food with such honesty, intelligence, and humor. She's an expert in one of life's greatest pleasures.

MOLLY'S STORY

Like every teenage girl in America, I labeled food "good" and "bad." Salad was good and M&M's were bad. I can remember being at my sixteenth birthday party, and my parents had bought me a beautiful cake. I was on the Weight Watchers program at the time. Since I was using food to deprive myself, I didn't eat a single slice of my own cake. I felt as though I'd be a bad person if I took a slice. For one year after that birthday, I didn't eat any cake whatsoever. Food was only healthy and helpful to me if I deprived myself of it. When I ate, I saw food only in terms of quantity. The more food there was, the more satisfied I thought I'd be.

Vanessa Marshall, the daughter of actress Joan Van Ark, knows how it feels to deprive herself of food. I met her on a model casting for a fashion shoot in California. She has explored her relationship with food and beauty as a comedian and writer. Her story begins with rebellion.

VANESSA'S STORY

For eleven months, I ate absolutely no carbohydrates. At that point in my life, I really felt that the outside of me would make me happy inside. I felt that if I just shrank my body enough, I would then feel comfortable on the planet. So I didn't go near any carbohydrates. I kept trying and trying to stay on the plan.

But there came a day when all hell broke loose. I was in New York for a weekend. I went to H & H Bagels on the West Side. Oh my God, I felt so naughty. I wanted to have an intimate relationship with these bagels. I ate one, smothered in cream cheese, then another and another. I made up for lost time. It was a carbohydrate love fest. I left the bagel shop and then found a shop selling muffins. And I remember combing the streets at four o'clock in the morning to find the perfect corn bread. After the day of eating all the carbohydrates I could sink my teeth into, I walked back to the hotel I was staying in, and I felt like I should be shot. I felt like I should just write out my will, bequeath my property, and die. Not only was I ashamed but I felt like I was a waste of life. I felt like I had no discipline and no value whatsoever.

In the darkest period of my life, I used food for comfort.

MY STORY

For two years, while away in London attending a dramatic arts school, I numbed myself out with food. I was across the ocean, away from the people I love dearly, and I lost all sense of myself. It was alienating to be one of the few Americans in a school consisting of English, Scottish, and Irish students. Food became my comfort. It never talks back in an unfamiliar dialect.

Peter, my professor, felt that although I was good at playing a role, I wasn't always *in* the role. I was an actor who was supposed to have studied at the University of Washington, but the graduate program had been shut down after I had been accepted there. The program in London was my consolation. I lacked focus because all I could think about was how much happier I would have been in Seattle.

With zero concentration, unable to remember my lines, I felt like a failure

in the one area where I had always excelled. Forgetting my lines was my worst nightmare. My professors arranged for me to see an "actors' " psychiatrist. His method was dream interpretation. I wasn't sleeping well at that point because I had put myself into what I would call a "food coma." My erratic schedule meant that I would grab dinner at eleven o'clock at night. I would return to my apartment in London and I would pick up a large pizza and eat it in my room by myself. I'd still feel terribly frustrated and alone. I'd sneak into the communal kitchen, pull out a large container of ice cream from the freezer, and take it back to my room. I finally finished eating at around 2:00 A.M. To hide the evidence, I would take the empty containers and boxes out to the garbage bins early the next morning before anyone in the house awoke.

I hated the feelings of numbness I woke up with each morning. And, like forgetting my lines, I failed to remember any of my dreams. Before each session, I flipped through a dream-interpretation book. Instead of using it to jog my memory, I used it to fabricate my dreams. I said that I had dreamed of overflowing bathtubs, being lost in a forest, and—the one I used most often—being buried alive. Through the deceit, I actually started having these dreams. It was then that I confessed all to the dream doctor. By this point, I was freaked out. He responded, "Michele, you have the power to control your actions with food in the same way that you have controlled telling me what dreams you said you had." I was hiding. Numbing myself out and making things up became my wake-up call.

I'd like you to tune in to your attitudes toward food.

➤ **TUNE IN**

In your Learning Curves journal, write down your first memory of food.

1. How old were you?

2. Who was there? Family members, friends, or were you by yourself?

3. Where were you? At home? In a restaurant? At a party?

4. What were the smells? The temperature of the room? The taste in your mouth?

5. Did you feel happy or sad?

6. Were you eating for comfort or celebration?

7. Do you have more than one memory?

Can you see a pattern?

➤ **LIVE OUT LOUD**

This exercise is designed to help you change your relationship with food.

take these steps:

1. Eat when you are hungry.

2. Create a time to sit down for a meal in your own home.

3. Try a new restaurant with friends and order something you've never tasted.

4. Keep a supply of your favorite foods you've been told you should not

eat at home. (I have found over the years that if I keep ice cream in the freezer and know it's there, I can have it when I want it. Having that food available, there is less chance of feeling the need to eat it all at once.)

5. Remember that the word *guilty* only applies to criminal behavior and not to eating.

In *When Women Stop Hating Their Bodies,* Jane R. Hirschmann and Carol H. Munter say, "Eating when you are hungry means breaking with the tradition of eating three meals a day. The scheduling of meals three times a day evolved from the needs of the workplace rather than the needs of the body. Eating has been determined by a time clock rather than by your own biological clocks. You need to rediscover your own individual 'eating clock'—and that means giving up meals in favor of eating experiences each time you are hungry."

LEARNING CURVE 13

FOOD IS FUEL

So if food isn't related to your self-esteem and doesn't make you less or more of a person, what is food? First and foremost, food is fuel. Remember, like a car, your body needs to have a smooth-running engine in order to get you from point A to point B. You need to have the energy to get through your life. How can we do that when the engine's cranky and wants to stay parked? Food is the fuel that keeps us going. My question for you is this: How do you fuel your body?

It's important to develop a relationship with food that mirrors the one you have with your car. For example, your car may work best on unleaded gasoline. You go to the gas station, choose the gas, put it in, and drive off. You know that your car doesn't work as well on diesel fuel. It's the same with your body. Just as your car works better on a certain type of gas, your body works better on certain fuels. I ask you to think about what foods fuel your body. It's amazing how a change in attitude will shift your relationship with food. Making choices that don't deny or deprive you, but give you what you need, will ultimately help give you the freedom to energize your body and take the mental pressure away from your judgments about food.

WENDY'S STORY

After years in therapy and on various diets, I now take the perspective that *I* make the decisions on what goes in me. Nobody else does. There was no epiphany, but I do know that living on my own makes me accountable to myself instead of to my parents. I used to think that the checkout lady was evaluating what I was buying, and now I just can't be bothered worrying about that. I am learning to be strong and confident enough to stop feeling that people are watching what I order when I'm in a restaurant. I am proud to say it: I eat dessert! I love it! I could care less if the waiter goes back to the kitchen and says to the chef, "See that fat woman at table thirty-four? She's ordered raspberry cheesecake." I've had to give up the fantasy that people talk about me in regard to my food if I am ever to understand that nothing is terrible and I'm not terrible for choosing to eat that cheesecake. It's a life lesson that I'm learning. Food is whatever you make it.

MOLLY'S STORY

In my early twenties I became a chef. That's when I changed my attitudes toward food and found freedom within myself. As I studied the ingredients and prepared the meals, I developed a deep appreciation for food. Today, I look at food in terms of quality and achievement. My palate has also developed and I realize the complexity of our palates. If I desire something salty and crispy, my first response is not to reach for the potato chips. There are other ways and different choices to make food serve me and give my body what it requests. I don't approach the table with a negative attitude. Food is a wonderful experience and I am learning to keep building my palate database.

VANESSA'S STORY

Since the no-carb diet, I've been vegan, macrobiotic, done the Atkins diet, and every food plan you can imagine. Mecca was nowhere to be found by looking outside of myself for the answers. I had to look within. After that bagelfest and all the food plans, I realized that I would never do anything based on someone else telling me that I can't. What I've come around to is to give myself the permission to eat whatever I want whenever I want, but I have learned that moderation is a beautiful concept. I honestly believe that God put food on the planet for me to enjoy. I celebrate food, and when I approach the refrigerator with a feeling of gratitude and celebration, I find that I don't have the time or the room inside me for judgment. I realize that I have good instincts. And I trust them. I have truly learned to be compassionate with myself and forgiving. I don't have any rules and I always make choices consciously. What my body is meant to be is based on me listening to what it asks me for.

MY STORY

After my experience in London, it became clear that for most of my life I had been eating on the sly, numbing myself from my own feelings and hiding food. I can remember the first time moving into my own apartment in New York and filling the refrigerator with all the things I wanted. My mother wouldn't be able to open my refrigerator, my brother wouldn't take my Doritos, and my sister wouldn't take my Fudgsicle bars. I realized that I owned my food, bought with my own money, and no one was going to take it away from me. There was no rush to inhale the contents of my refrigerator in the quickest amount of time.

In order to learn a healthy way to look at food, I saw a nutritionist, Dr. Sheri Lieberman. She analyzed my eating patterns and told me that there was no right way for everyone, but we needed to find the best way for me. My metabolism is such that I need to feed myself regularly. We're told that there's breakfast, lunch, and dinner. But she told me that I am better off having smaller meals five to six times a day, so that my energy level stays constant.

One night at dinner, I realized that if I didn't want to finish all the food on my plate because I was actually full, I could take it home or I could leave it. There suddenly became no hurry to eat something, no pressure to finish it. I had a choice to decide what I would eat and when I would eat it. I started to pay attention to when I was truly hungry. I began to notice that there were times that I didn't need to have a full-course meal but, rather, wanted something lighter than my friends were ordering.

As I listened to the signals that indicated whether I craved something savory or sweet, my nutritionist began to teach me that food is fuel. She explained how I would feel when I ate carbohydrates (which slow me down) and sugar (which temporarily speeds me up.) She taught me to see how certain foods would help me get fueled up and energized to live my life. I started to look at the positive effects of eating more vegetables and fruits, and proteins.

Learning what will make me feel better has been a huge process. I feel better if I have protein in the morning (eggs, yogurt, or cottage cheese) as opposed to a lot of carbohydrates (bagels, French toast, or pancakes). If I want dessert, I'll have it. It doesn't have to be a conversation with myself. Although my work means that I'm often out at social functions, I love to cook. And, yes, pizza is still my favorite food and I don't deny myself the pleasure once in a while. Isn't food better for us when we eat with conscious choice?

To be able to enjoy all the things I love, I use the method of a food guide pyramid from the U.S. Department of Agriculture/U.S. Department of Health and Human Services. Eating grains, then lots of fruits and vegetables, followed by proteins, then milk products, and finally fats, oils, and sweets in smaller moderation works for me. I still choose to have a sweet for dessert once in a while or a drink with dinner. I had to start somewhere, and this has been as good a place as any for me. No rules on the right fish or the perfect pasta. I've used common sense and my own inner signals for learning how and when to fuel myself. In the process, I have found food freedom.

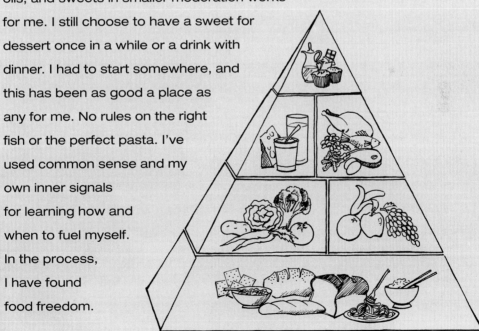

Now it's time for you to tune in.

> **TUNE IN**

In your Learning Curves journal, write a list of foods in each group on the pyramid that you love. Now, write another list of foods you feel that you should not eat that appeal to you. Give yourself permission to have these. This will form a grocery list of foods you enjoy. Enough said.

> **LIVE OUT LOUD**

Take these steps to build your own food guide pyramid.

1. *Be realistic.* Make small changes over time in what you eat and the level of activity you do. After all, small steps work better than giant leaps. Modify your food choices gradually. That may be easier than overhauling your whole diet at one time.
2. *Be sensible.* Enjoy all foods, just don't overdo it. Choose foods each day from the five major food groups. Build your pyramid from the bottom up—with plenty of grains, proteins, fruits, and vegetables.
3. *Be adventurous.* Expand your tastes to enjoy a variety of foods. Go for variety within food groups. Besides the nutritional benefits, variety adds interest to meals and snacks.
4. *Be flexible.* Go ahead and balance what you eat and the physical activity you do over several days. No need to worry about just one meal or one day. Make moderation, not elimination, your goal. Eat foods

lower in fat and sugars more often than those that have more. And trade off to keep your meals and snacks in balance.

The Food Guide Pyramid pamphlet, developed by the International Food Information Council Foundation in Washington, D.C., can help you make healthy choices that fit your lifestyle so you can do the things you want to do.

LEARNING CURVE 14

EXERCISE MAKES YOU FIT, NOT THIN

Rochelle Rice, M.A., president and founder of In Fitness & In Health (200 E. 35th Street, Suite 2, New York, 212-688-4558, www.infitnessinhealth.com), New York's only fitness studio for women of size, says, "The greatest goal of any fitness program for a woman of size is to overcome social barriers with regard to exercise. 'I lead an active lifestyle' will become the answer to the phrase 'do not work out.' A life filled with physical activity will become the success of the next century."

Getting to the gym was definitely harder for me in college than doing the exercise itself. It wasn't always on my agenda as a "must" and I rarely remembered how good I felt after I'd spent even half an hour moving my body. But, as you read our stories, you will see how we have learned that exercise doesn't have to be torture, doesn't have to be at the gym, and is surely one of the ways to feel good about oneself. As Rochelle points out, "There is a collective consciousness with regard to women and movement. There is this surge of energy happening where women are beginning to understand that *all* movement is good. Fitness does not equal thin, nor does it mean having to hit the traditional gym three to five times per week at 85 percent maximal heart rate. As each woman finds her unique ability to move, she frees the path for another to join her."

WENDY'S STORY

What gets me going to the gym? Mostly habit. I've done it on and off for years. Hopefully more on than off. I feel better eating whatever it is I'm eating if I'm exercising regularly. It provides a good balance. Plus, rumor has it that there are huge medical benefits to exercise, so why not go with the flow?

When I walk on the treadmill, I finish feeling exhilarated and exhausted. Usually, I like walking to a destination. I don't consider myself to be a nature lover, so the thought of a walk through a field doesn't inspire me. I realize that I'm never going to be an Oprah exerciser, up at 4:30 in the morning to run up a mountain. But what I do, and I exercise regularly, gives me a sense of accomplishment. I give myself the big thumbs-up and feel that I am making an investment in my body. I relax about my body issues and just take pride in what I'm doing for myself.

MOLLY'S STORY

I was a competitive swimmer as a child and have always seen the value of exercise. I did the whole aerobics routine, but it wasn't until my thirties that I really found my perfect exercise. I started hiking up mountains. It was wonderful and made me feel good about how I was caring for my body. At forty years old, however, I developed a series of health problems connected to pregnancy, which meant that there were certain forms of exercise I couldn't do. I found it difficult to get back into a routine. I realize that my body cannot take high-impact exercise such as a forty-five-minute run on the treadmill. I don't run up mountains anymore, but walk up them. Even though I've learned that my body needs to be exercised differently, I still enjoy a rigorous walk. I still enjoy the *exercise* of exercise.

VANESSA'S STORY

Without sounding like Jane Fonda, I love exercise. First, I love to dance. I express myself through movement and I feel so sexy. All women have the power to feel fabulous when they dance. I also kick-box. It's like a violent ballet. I see it as a dance movement because it's somewhat choreographed and precise. When I go to the gym and they turn up the music, and I beat the living crap out of one of those bags, I honestly leave there feeling like I could do anything. I feel so empowered.

Listen to me: It *never* used to be like that. Before, it was a treachery that I had to go to the gym. I grew up in a household where my parents ran seven miles a day come hell or high water, and they would offer me new wardrobes if I would just go running with them. Subtle bribes like that made me think, If I don't exercise, there's really something wrong with me. So I would either exercise to please them or not exercise to rebel against them. I'd say, "I will not do what you want me to do!" When I got to NYU, I'd get up at 6:00 A.M., run five miles, and sleep through class. I think it was out of guilt. I also joined a gym. For me, going to the gym, running on the treadmill, and sitting on the bike were all so boring. All I had to think about was that I had to burn this many calories and get my heart rate into this zone in order to get into fat burning. I'll never forget the day I was sitting on the exercise bike at the gym, wishing that I could be anyplace else. I saw a kick-boxing class going on and the teacher was a Native American woman who was so beautiful and so powerful. I got off the bike and went up to her. "What's the deal with the kick-boxing?" I said. The teacher told me that she does it because she really loves her body. I signed up immediately. I've learned that the process of exercise, which in my case is kick-boxing, is far more important than the results. It's such a joy. I go out dancing once a week, and although I'm sure dancing burns calories, too, that's not the point of it. I just do what's fun.

MY STORY

I used to see exercise as a chore. In grade school, I can remember being herded off to a softball field during phys ed. I hated the uniforms, let alone the fact that I was being forced to participate in a sport I wasn't good at. As I grew older, I had more choices in the sports I could hate. I swam for many years on a competitive team and skied with my school or family on weekends up north. No sport ever felt like my choice.

In college, my girlfriend and I joined a local health club. It was all treadmills and StairMasters. That wasn't good for my shinsplints. Neither was the step class, with an instructor who made me move so quickly up and down a set of steps to 1980s music, I thought I would have coronary arrest by the time the hour was over. So much for that.

I was on exercise hiatus until I was introduced by a friend to strength-conditioning exercises. Most gyms offer these type of classes, but I could also do this activity at home. This gave me a chance to stretch and move my body in a controlled way that didn't feel like torture. I then began to believe that there were other ways to exercise that I could enjoy. I realized that doing some sort of exercise gave me downtime. Away from my desk at work, I could check in with myself and even destress. I could unplug and recharge.

I have learned to see exercise as a gift, a form of self-love. My favorite part of exercising is appreciating what I'm doing for me. I realize that I want to take care of myself so that I outlive my parents. This new attitude has allowed me to embrace exercise. I even feel comfortable going to the gym. I realized that everyone there is only concerned about how *they* look. They're not even paying attention to me. Only *I* am paying myself the attention I feel I'm worth.

When you get out of the mind-set that, first, working out is for thin people and not for us; second, that the gym is a rigorous ordeal; and, third, that going to the gym is the only form of exercise, you can begin to see exercise as a strengthening of the mind as well as of the body. All forms of movement are great for our minds and our bodies. I'd like you to tune in to exercise.

➤ TUNE IN

I want you to do this visualization exercise. It was developed by Pat Lyons and Debby Burgard and taken from their wonderful book *Great Shape: The First Fitness Guide for Large Women* (San Francisco: Bull Publishing Company, 1990). I still use this technique to get in touch with what type of exercise my body needs.

This is a relaxation and visualization exercise designed to help you get to know your desire to move. It is easier to do if you have someone you trust read slowly to you while you close your eyes or tape-record yourself reading slowly and replay it with your eyes closed.

You can do this exercise more than once; in fact it can be a daily practice to help you identify what sort of movement you want.

First, lie down on a comfortable surface and loosen any constricted clothing so you can relax and breathe. Gently close your eyes and let your attention come to rest on your breathing. You are not trying to change your breathing, you are just noticing it, trusting that your breath will take care of itself. In and out, in and out, let your rhythm lull you.

Your breath washes through the blocked places in your body, and as you breathe out, it takes with it any tension. . . . Now begin at your feet and check each part of your body. . . . Move up to your ankles. . . . Move up to your knees and thighs. . . . Squeeze them and feel the pleasure of that warmth, then release. Move up to your buttocks. . . . Continue upward. . . . Feel the flow of relaxation moving through your body.

Your body is now warm and relaxed. What sort of movement to do you see in your mind at this time? Try on a few ideas. Imagine how your muscles would feel doing something. Slow and easy? Or do you need something stronger, something to pump heat? Smooth fluid motions? Or harder, tighter movements? Where in your body do you feel a readiness for hard work? Take a few moments to locate your desire.

Do you want this activity to be in water or on land? Do you want to move to music? Do you want fast or slow pacing? Steady or a variety? Do you want to be alone or with friends? Let your imagination call on every sense to paint a picture for you.

What do you see? What do you hear? What fragrance is in the air? Who is there?

Give yourself a few moments to really embellish the scene.

When you feel ready, let your attention return to your breath. Then slowly open your eyes.

You might want to write down your impressions or thoughts, or you can just reflect on what you envisioned.

The purpose is to take the time to check in with your physical self and get to know your feelings about movement. . . .

If you did come up with some images of the kind of movement you wanted, it may have surprised you, given what you thought up till now.

➤ LIVE OUT LOUD

As Rochelle recommends, the success of a fitness program should be measured by the following:

1. Does the fitness program increase the ease of your ADL (activities of daily living)? Climbing stairs, getting in and out of your car more easily, carrying your children or groceries?

2. Does the fitness program improve the quality of your life by enhancing your daily energy levels, decreasing your stress levels, and helping you to make the connection between your body and mind?

Using this criteria, begin to experiment until you find the right type of exercise for you. Consider some of the ideas that you got from the Tune In exercise. Start with something simple and then increase your activity level as you feel appropriate. Cinder Ernst feels there are two goals to aim for.

1. Show up: In order to show up, you have got to know what works for you and what doesn't. Take note of what you like to do.
2. Enjoy the ride: If it doesn't feel good, you need to change it; so you need to be present and aware of how you feel.

Here are three levels of activity ranging from gentler to more strenuous movement. Only you can determine what level works for you.

LEVEL 1 EXAMPLES

Walk instead of drive when you can.

Take the stairs instead of the elevator.

Go to a dance . . . and dance.

Participate on the company bowling team.

LEVEL 2 EXAMPLES

Enroll in a stretch class.

Walk for a specific amount of time on a treadmill or outside on a track.

Bicycle indoors or out.

Try an exercise video featuring a beginner's yoga class.

Take a more strenuous class like Pilates or karate.

Enroll in a dance class: Try jazz, hip-hop, funk.

Try a low-intensity weight-training program.

Work out with a personal trainer whose focus is health and well-being.

If you're thinking about working with a personal trainer, Cinder Ernst urges you to consider three points:

1. *You* are hiring *them.*
2. They can do what *you* want to do.
3. You are your own best expert—*be that.*

Remember, exercise is not just a means to lose weight, but your body depends on you to energize it. Open your mind to the possibility that exercise is an opportunity for you to take care of yourself. Exercise will allow you to learn something about yourself. Challenge yourself. Discover your power, strength, endurance, and agility.

LEARNING CURVE 15

YOUR WORDS HAVE POWER— LEARN TO USE THEM WISELY

How good is your body language? No, I'm not talking about your ability to send off all the right signals in a bar. What I mean is, how well do you speak of your body? Sure, people have been rude and unkind to us and we've felt crushed. As we enter the twenty-first century, fat is surely the last taboo. A person can be an alcoholic, a drug user, or violent, and they are treated with empathy. Someone can make fat jokes on Jay Leno's show or *Saturday Night Live,* but if they were to make gay, black, or misogynist jokes, there would be an outcry. The truth is that fat jokes aren't funny. We're such an easy target of hostility. The jokes are obvious, cruel, and downright insulting.

What about the language you use to describe yourself? Remember, everything you do is a reflection of everything you think and say about yourself. Can you honestly expect others to treat you well if you don't treat yourself well with the words that you use? It's so important to empower yourself with a vocabulary that reflects who you are, rather than disempowering yourself with a language consisting of self-deprecation. Just as you are learning to get comfortable with your body, it's time to get comfortable with the language you use to describe yourself.

Perhaps you describe yourself according to the current language used by everybody else. When Camryn Manheim accepted her Emmy by saying, "This is for all the fat girls," Camryn attempted to defuse the word *fat*. She used it to claim a word so often used as a threat, aimed at us by others. She mocked the cultural ideal that the word *fat* is a way of putting ourselves down and that it connotes self-loathing. By using the word *fat* to describe herself, she empowered herself. "Look," she cried, "I can use it, too!" I believe that her comment was intended for all the women who are being true to themselves. We all have described ourselves based on the language of others, the language we've inherited from society. Can you take the same language and use it to empower yourself, or do you need to look at changing your vocabulary?

WENDY'S STORY

When I watched Camryn accept her award, I started crying. I thought, I wanna be fat like her. I shouted into the TV screen, "I'll have what she's having!" I felt liberated. Lately, I've really wanted to work in TV. For the first time ever, I didn't think, I can't be on TV because I'm too fat. I'm thinking, if anyone says to me, "You're too fat to be on TV," my response will be, "Did you tell Camryn Manheim that, because she has an Emmy and a Golden Globe? Did you mention that to Rosie O'Donnell, Roseanne, Kathy Najimy, and Oprah? The biggest women on TV are the biggest women."

I now have more chutzpah. I have less to lose—literally. It just finally seemed easier to come out as a fat woman. At some point, the pressure of thinking that everyone in the whole wide world hated me or was going to make fun of me or talk about me behind my back became more intense than the fear of walking out there and saying, "I'm fat." So I did it. I came out. I call myself fat, and then take away anyone else's power to call me that. It's like saying, "Fine, tell me something I don't know. I'm the one in my skin; I'm the one in my life. Now go bother someone else."

When I choose my body vocabulary, I'm careful not to sound like a Hallmark card. You know, "voluptuous and zaftig." It doesn't say what I mean. My favorite word is *gifted.* When I look at myself in the mirror, I say, "I honestly don't see how this is a problem for some people. Why do people feel threatened because of this?" To me, it was a huge statement about plus-size women that Bill Clinton, the current president of the United States, arguably the most powerful man in the entire world, picked a "fat chick." If someone hasn't seen me and we arrange to meet in a café, I have to describe myself. The first time I met Michele, I described myself as a "big girl, black hair, shaped like a china doll, red lips, dark nails, white skin." I say "big girl" a lot. I'm trying to let go of the negative connotations some words have because of the way they've been used against us. I mean, they're just words.

It is possible to take the word *fat* and own it if you feel it accurately describes who you are. Finding a language that supports who you are is a process of discovery. Try the words on, as it were, and feel if they fit. More often than not, we search for a vocabulary different from the existing language or create one that turns the current language on its head.

VANESSA'S STORY

I think I have found a positive way to talk about myself. It comes from a place of not being angry. I no longer feel ashamed for being larger and upset for being tortured as a kid. For years, I would say affirmations like "I love myself unconditionally." I think it had a cumulative effect over time, but what I did find was that I needed to ask better questions, like "How can I feel better about myself and what do I have to be grateful for today?" They were things that induced a thought, word, or action. I am now a stand-up comedian in Los Angeles, and the best way to describe myself is through the vehicle of humor. It's funny how my ass has become my franchise. It's an unwritten rule that "perfect" people aren't allowed to be funny. You're either butt-ugly, gay, or angry and people find you funny. But if you're mildly intelligent, somewhat sophisticated, and beautiful, you're going to have a hard time getting the audience to like you. I don't know why. My material has changed over time. I started out talking about human evil, why children are so mean, and the dark side of humanity. And, yes, I would talk about my body. I'd tell people that I starved my body in order to become the perfect skeleton. What I realize is that my body has turned out to be a gift. My intention is to celebrate myself and come from a place of love, not fear. If I couldn't laugh at myself, I'd go mad. I describe myself today as *"phat."* I am all that and more. I am awesome. But people think I'm saying the word *fat*. They say, "How can you talk about yourself like that?" I also call *phat* modeling "waddling." It makes fun of the idea that there's another branch of modeling. I'm not being mean or endorsing a negative idea of myself. I think it's fantastic. I think I'm all that—I'm *phat*.

When you choose a language that best describes you, free from anger and hurt, you are able to express who you are with the power of words. Always choose words that empower you, words that make you feel good. As you get comfortable in your skin, the words you choose will reflect the positive thoughts you have about yourself.

MOLLY'S STORY

I have two thoughts on my own body language. The first is how I describe myself to myself and the second is how other people hopefully describe me. When describing myself, I don't feel the need to refer to my size. It's not important. The words that I would use are *tall, brunette, athletic, midwestern, successful,* and *the perpetual big sister.* I'm a very American woman. Of course, the words I use to describe myself depend on how I feel that day. One day I may refer to myself as an "aging slob" and the next as "at the peak of my highest potential."

How you feel about yourself on any given day affects how you treat yourself with the words you use. It's amazing how different you can sound when you're having a feel-good day as opposed to a not so good day. You should aim to feel at the peak of your highest potential every day or at least recognize your potential and strive toward it. It's not easy when our lives are difficult and stressful. As you think about how you describe yourself, what would you say about yourself to a total stranger who has never seen you?

MY STORY

Describing myself to a stranger was the perfect time for me to paint a picture of myself in words. I had responded to a personal ad in *New York* magazine. I listened to the messages of several guys just to hear their voices. One guy sounded as if he smoked two packs a day; one sounded dry, another dull, and then there was the man who sounded cute. He described himself well. He spoke well of himself. I left a message on his voice mail, and within a couple of days, he returned my call. His name was Bobby. He and I spoke six times before eventually meeting for a date. But it wasn't until we had agreed to meet that Bobby asked me what I looked like. Until that point, I had shown him my true self: my humor, my interests, and my unique take on life. In reply to his question, I said, "I'm a big girl with a pretty face and great legs." That was the first time that I had verbalized my appearance to someone else, an interested stranger. And we had the first of many wonderful dates. I realized that how I spoke of myself was as important for him to hear as it was when I listened to his initial description of himself. Speaking well of myself, no frills, no lies, freed me from every hurtful word uttered by anyone else and created an opening for me to share what I have and who I am with another person.

Although we are often at the mercy of someone else's words, we have the power to create our own vocabulary. It's important that you choose words that reflect who you are. Humor is a great way to get comfortable with your body. So, too, is honesty. Always come from a place of love. Remember, what you say about your body affects how you feel about yourself.

Today, tune in to your body language.

➤ **TUNE IN**

Think about how you describe your body every day. What words do you use and, more importantly, how do they make you feel? Look at the words cited below and write down the ones you choose the most often.

Big, full-figured, large, overweight, plus-size, heavy, round, supple, soft, fleshy, fat, phat, strong, curvy, voluptuous, sexy, pear-shaped, Rubenesque, athletic, grand, zaftig, proportionate, beautiful, striking, impressive, unique, powerful.

If you've chosen negative words, like *overweight* (to which I would respond, "Over what weight?"), think about the positive ways you can describe your body.

➤ **LIVE OUT LOUD**

Now that you've chosen the words that you feel accurately and positively describe your body and physical appearance, I want you to write your own personal ad in your Learning Curves journal. Speak well of yourself. Read how you've presented yourself on paper. Starting today, make a commitment to yourself that you'll use only the words that make you feel good about yourself.

Your body language is essential for you to respect your body and "own" your own skin. People may put you down and their words may sometimes hurt. But remember, their words will hurt much less once you get comfortable with the body you have. Your body language gives you the power to realize that if someone says anything negative to you or about you, it's *their* issue. It's something inside them that they haven't dealt with. Try not to make it *your* issue. You make it your issue only if you say something negative about yourself. You're worth far more than buying into someone else's problem. Create your own path to happiness and never seek to stand in your own way.

A NOTE ON STEPS 5 AND 6

As I'm sure you know by now, this book is here to help you discover yourself from the inside out. Your style within gives you your style on the outside. We have looked back at the past, looked inside ourselves, and looked at our bodies. Now we're going to look at what goes on the body. These next steps begin your journey to find and express your outer style. This is where the real fun begins! Take the journey with me to enter a place where the worlds of inner style and clothes combine. Join me in the search for your outer style.

As a woman who has worked in fashion for the last twelve years, starting as a temp and working my way up to becoming a fashion and style director, I have learned a lot about clothes in the full-figured market. I have helped to create and nurture the market so that we can find clothes to suit our needs and tastes. You are in safe hands. Let's begin the journey.

Refining Your Style

You are who you are. Show your face. Develop your own style. Don't go by anyone else's in the magazines. Take a piece here and a piece there. Make it your own. Steal from nature, steal from art, and steal from music.

YVETTE FREEMAN, ACTOR

YOUR OUTWARD APPEARANCE IS A REFLECTION OF YOUR INNER STYLE

We've talked at length about finding who you are and how you feel on the inside. Now we are going to step outside. What have clothes got to do with your past, your inner style, your body, and your attitude about mind over matter? The answer: A lot.

Outer style, your visual representation, starts by remembering your inner reflection. Step 2 began that journey. Take a moment to reread your journal. Now that you have remembered who *you* are today, it's important that you express yourself through clothes. What do you say about yourself when you walk into a room without having uttered a word? Your style whispers the answer. As you know, style is not just about clothes. Style is about self-definition, attitude, and the way you feel. It's not always about being noticed, but being remembered. Style comes from within. It's a philosophy—your way of being.

Think of some women who have style. Maria Callas, Marilyn Monroe, and Coco Chanel conjure up very different and yet very distinct images of style. They didn't just wear it; they exuded it. What is it about them that made them style icons? The answer is that their inner style was truly reflected on the outside. They wore what they were. From the dramatic to the sexy and the classic, their self-definition is what makes the world remember them. *Your* style is who *you* are. How are you remembered?

Often, *fashion* is used as a synonym for *style.* We mistake one for the other. Fashion is fleeting, while style endures. Fashion is uniform; style is individual. Fashion dictates; style empowers. Fashion is impulse; style is instinct. Fashion follows trends; style follows taste. Fashion is self-serving; style serves the self. Dress your self.

Personal style acknowledges who you are. Expresses who you are. Celebrates who you are. The journey to find your style, as these women's stories attest, begins with a feeling, lives in exposure, and ends with a reflection—a mirror image of their inner style.

Audrey Smaltz is the most divalike woman I know. She started her career as a model. In 1982, she started her own business, the Ground Crew, which runs the backstage production for fashion shows for Donna Karan, Bill Blass, and Calvin Klein, among others. She lectures across the country on style for professional organizations and has developed her own accessory line, which she sells on QVC. Audrey is bold, stunning, irreverent, impeccable. She is the only woman, other than the writer herself, Maya Angelou, who can deliver the poem "Phenomenal Woman" with such force and truth.

AUDREY'S STORY

For me, style is the way I carry it; it's the way I feel about myself. I think, Tall, elegant, graceful. I think, Honey, I know I look good! My style is Harlem flash with Madison Avenue class. I learned style from my father. He was the best-dressed man in Harlem. I grew up in the first public housing development in the United States for colored folk. I never saw it as a "project." The buildings were four stories high, with tennis courts, pools, laundry rooms, and places to keep our bikes.

I didn't know I was poor. My father was a post office clerk. Every day, he went to work in a good suit, shirt, tie, cuff links, and polished shoes. For every suit, he had two pairs of pants, because the pants always wore out before the jacket. He'd go downtown to Orchard Street to buy squares of linen and cotton and he'd hand-stitch his handkerchiefs. My father taught me how to walk. Every Sunday night, we'd go for our walk around Harlem. I would wear my father's shirts with my own skirts and a pair of loafers. I felt fabulous. That's my style today.

For every Easter and Palm Sunday, I had my clothes made to order. *Made to order!* My mother played cards with Miss Grant, a seamstress who made clothes for all the wealthy women on Fifth Avenue. She bought the fabric and Miss Grant made my clothes. As a teenager, I had art, music, and dancing lessons, which cost fifty cents each. Expensive when you consider that my father brought home thirty dollars a month. But boy, was I exposed to the arts. My teacher, Mrs. Brighting, a beautiful white woman with a crooked wig and a wooden leg, exposed me to *National Geographic.* I'd look at the pictures and say to myself, I gotta go there one day. The library in the housing development was where you'd find me. All those pretty pictures. On Saturdays, I took the number 2 bus downtown and got off at Fifty-seventh Street. Tiffany's. I learned about diamonds, pearls, and table settings. When I buy, I'd say to myself, it will only be at this store. I went to charm school at fifteen, and entered the Ebony Fashion Fair. I'd sit on a chair, cross my legs, and people would *scream*! I've never taken fashion seriously. My philosophy today has always been the same: Just because it's *in* doesn't mean *I* have to be *in it.*

Finding your personal style gives you the confidence to be yourself. Think, Attitude. Think, Tall. Think, Wow! While the winds of fashion blow differently each season, your style is constant and stands the storms of passing trends. Audrey is a woman of style. Embracing who she is inside gives her the style she has outside. Knowing who she is and how she feels about herself allows Audrey's style to serve herself. Like birds in a nest, we first circle around the style of our parents, then fly off to all that is new to us—books, shops, and countries afar—before coming home to who we truly are. Style is an art form. It is the art of painting our canvas with the brush we hold inside.

Yvette Freeman is an actress on the hit show *ER* and is currently making her directing debut with *A Blessing Way.* I was privileged to meet Yvette during rehearsals of the stage show *Dinah Was,* in which she played the lead. We shot her for an issue of *Mode.* Helping to dress her for the fashion spread was joyful and fun, as I saw a woman sexy and free in her body. As a size eighteen, she is able to embrace her sensuality and uses it onstage to great effect.

YVETTE'S STORY

My mother is one of the most stylish women I've ever met. More stylish than any woman I've seen in a magazine. It comes from the way she walks, talks, and carries herself. She expected her girls to do the same. My classic style comes from my mother, my Afro-centric flair comes from my background, my casual look comes from the comfort I feel within myself, and the clean-cut lines come from knowing my own taste. I feel beautiful. I feel beautiful as Dinah Washington onstage, on the set of *ER,* and in the arms of my husband. I know it sounds like a cliché, but when I got married, I felt like the most beautiful woman in the world. Unable to find a gown that expressed who I am, I designed my own. It was a classic ivory dress with clean lines, which enhanced all my assets, and it fit to perfection. In *People*'s Best Gowns of 1996, mine was one of them. Mine, out of all those rich divas! Where does my style come from? I steal from nature, art, and music. They are my tools, my instruments. I can't be copied. My style is my own. I own it.

You buy fashion, but you own style. When we become a slave to fashion trends, we lose our sense of style. Attempting to look the same as everyone else, we forget that it's what makes us different that gives us our style. We've all had fashion faux pas. Audrey's was a heavily pleated skirt, Yvette's was a brown silk suit with dark sweat patches under the armholes, and mine was the grunge look worn in the nineties, which to this day makes me cringe. I'm sure you remember yours. They were faux pas because they weren't true to our individual style. We learn by experience what makes us feel good and best reflects who we are. We are inspired by art, music, books, and dance. Expose yourself to the beauty of nature and your beauty within in order to find and express your own beauty as a woman of style. Remember, magazines dictate which clothes they think we should be wearing. We've listened and paid for our mistakes. But it's always our own style that gives us our sense of self.

MY STORY

As a child, I coveted clothes. I fell in love with the movie *Funny Face,* collected Huk-A-Poo blouses, and read about the Hollywood women then in style. But one occasion stands out as the day I found and expressed my personal style. It was the day of my brother Steven's bar mitzvah. I was sixteen and we lived in a middle-class, mainly Jewish suburb of Detroit. I found the person I was meant to be. Fall's breeze had started to blow the crisp leaves from the trees. They fell every-where—on manicured lawns, freshly painted porches, and in the gutters. My mother had taken me shopping two weeks prior to Steven's big day. We traipsed around every shop, trundled through every department store, scanned every rack, and sought every color. We bought nothing because neither of us could agree: I wanted something young yet sophisticated; my mother wanted to cover me up. Exhausted from looking at every garment in Michigan, my mother eventually chose a wet sand–colored angora sweater and a long, slim skirt. I gave in. The items remained folded in the handsome shopping bag in which they had left the store. I put the bag at the foot of my closet—untouched, unopened.

It was bar mitzvah morning and I heard the audible buzz of jubilant aunts and congratulatory grandmothers vibrating from downstairs. I dressed slowly. Pulling the sweater out of its bag and over my head dampened my spirits. I itched. Next out of the bag was the skirt my mother had assured me looked fine. Last came the heels. Hesitantly, I turned to look at myself in the full-length mirror. "Who are you?" I asked my reflection in the mirror. I wanted to sink through the floor. The girl in the mirror looked sixty, not sixteen, weighed 120 kilos, not 120 pounds, and resembled the rabbi's wife, not the brother's sister. It was me, and I felt dreadful.

Just then, my mother knocked. "We're all waiting for you," she called out. When I heard her footsteps glide away, I tiptoed out. There was no way I was ready to greet my family. I entered my mother's closet, and at a glance, I lifted two hangers, then hastily returned to my room. Off went the ill-fitting skirt, which lay like a dishcloth on the thick pile carpet. I pulled a tweed skirt off my clothes rack, box-pleated and very pretty, which fastened effortlessly around the waist and fell to the knee. I felt better. But my top still looked like a hairy sand castle. Off it went. I put on a cream silk blouse I had raided from my mother's closet—one she had never worn. I buttoned it down. Much better. Finally, my mother's Carole Little chocolate brown velvet blazer completed the style challenge. Heels back on, I stood in front of the mirror. There I was. My inner style radiated out. Although some were my mother's clothes, she would never have worn them that way. I made the clothes reflect *my* style. The outfit was stamped with my own flair: wooden Candie's slingbacks, mauve nails, a crocheted long scarf, my trademark ring, bracelet, and watch, and small hoop earrings.

My personal style hasn't changed since. I still like the simplicity of line and shape because it allows for my personality to color the canvas. Nothing is more stylish than effortless dressing, because when we look as though we've tried too hard, we've given the game away.

I'd like you to tune in to finding your personal style.

➤ TUNE IN

Find new sources of inspiration. Style isn't limited to just a dress or a suit; it is inspired by everything around you.

take these steps:

1. Promise yourself that for the next two weeks you won't buy any new clothing (it's a tough one!).

2. Temporarily stop reading the magazines you always read.

3. Shut off the old flow of information.

4. Set some time aside to go to a bookstore and browse through art and photography books.

5. Pick up several new magazines: on gardening, food, and travel. Buy the new magazines that look really interesting to you.

6. Cut out images of color, shape, form, and flavor. Make a collage.

7. Describe in your Learning Curves journal what attracts your attention. Begin to get a sense of your taste through the images that catch your eye.

➤ **LIVE OUT LOUD**

I'd like you to go into a clothing store, one that you haven't been into before. What clothes catch your eye? Are you noticing that you're attracted to certain shapes and colors like those in the images you've collected? Remember, it's not a trip to buy. You may not fully realize what your personal style is because you've spent so long living by other people's dictates. That's okay. Closing the usual flow of information gives you the opportunity to find out for yourself. Your openness and instincts will lead you to find and express your true style. Exposure to new colors, different shapes, textures, and designs gives you the power to dress yourself as you are. Begin to find and refine your style. Embody the style that is uniquely you.

LEARNING CURVE 17

You Have to Get Rid of the Old to Make Way for the New . . . You

You may not have realized it, but you've probably been living with more than one woman. They're all in your closet. Your closet is emblematic of a former self, testament to all the sizes you have been or hope to be, and may inaccurately describe the woman you are right now. And of course, there are all the "one day, I'll get myself back into that" clothes. Think about what's in your closet. Is any part of *you* buried among the boxes?

Yes and no. There are pieces that still make your heart race: the suit you wore for your daughter's wedding, the fabulous bag you found marked down at a store, the shoes that make you feel drop-dead gorgeous every time you wear them, and, of course, the top drawer filled with your favorite lingerie. And then there's *everything* else: the other suits, which don't fit and are the shade of green you liked *last* year; the other bags, worn down from their years of use; the other shoes, which pinch your feet every time your wear them; and the faded cotton panties that you feel will just do. And I can't forget what you've forgotten—that is, every other piece of clothing that hasn't seen the light of day in the last year.

These are the women who live in your closet. They've all had lives, and though many of them have long been over, you've allowed them to continue living with you. Constant reminders of the way you were or wanted to be and the life they led with you. It's important to release the skeletons, the clothes that no longer reflect who you are. "Oh my God," I hear you cry, "she's going to ask me to get rid of everything I own!" No, I'm not. That is, unless everything you have does not reflect who you are. What I am saying is that you should think about owning a closet that mirrors your true self and makes you say, "That's me! That's me!" every time you open it. I promise you that you'll never again have to say, "I have nothing to wear."

AUDREY'S STORY

I used to have a huge closet. Dozens of shoes, different styles, in different shapes, colors, and sizes. The sizes in my closet ranged from ten to twenty-two. That all changed when I realized that my inner style meant being organized and that I didn't want long discussions over what I would

wear each day. So I began to give away all the clothes that didn't express who I am. The good pieces went into storage, ready for New York's FIT (Fashion Institute of Technology) museum. They're just too perfect. My twenty-two-year-old niece and sister-in-law wait for what they call my "hand-me-ups." I give everything away as I go along. Now I have a small closet. I wear everything in it because all my pieces mirror my needs and express who I am. I realize that I don't need a big closet. I see my friends' closets, where the shoes have become part of the bedroom decor because they can't remember what they have. They have so many shoes! I like that I know all my pieces of clothing.

What's the point of hunting through the jumble to find the outfit we wore years ago? Worse, we find it, put it on, look in the mirror, and face the shock: Who's this middle-aged woman and why is she in *my* room? Depression strikes as we toss the outfit back into the closet. We forget that our bodies and tastes have changed with the passing of time. If you don't claim a closet that reflects who you are today, the past life that one of your ladies led will come back to haunt you.

YVETTE'S STORY

I'm guilty of having a size wardrobe. Now, very happy as a size eighteen, my closet runs the size gamut. I used to find it hard to clear my closet to make way for who I am. You see, some of the clothes are real nice. But I realized that I didn't wear half of what I had. My closet was full of clothes that the TV shows I work on let me keep. Although the clothes were beautiful, they were what my characters wore. They weren't what I would wear. So, one day, I opened my closet, took a deep breath, said into it, "This is who I am," and began to take the clothes that didn't reflect my style out of the closet and put them on my bed. Of course, there was the "Shall I/shouldn't I" discussion, and some of the clothes almost made it back into the closet. But as I kept reclaiming who I am, I found myself with a huge pile of clothes on the bed, and an edited collection of clothes in my closet. All the clothes I loved. All the clothes that were me.

It's so important to have a closet that reflects your style. Clearing the closet is like clearing the mind and airing the soul. As Yvette said, it allows room for you to express who you are effortlessly. You'll find that every piece will work together. Editing your closet relieves the anxiety of wondering what to wear and whether you'll fit into it. This is truly refining your style. Choose to keep the pieces that make you feel great. Give away the rest; in so doing, you're giving someone else the opportunity to find and express their style, now that you have found yours.

MY STORY

I've spent much of my life's work finding the trends, editing photo shoots, and editing the clothes we choose to photograph. But when it came to editing my own closet, I had no idea how to do it. My closet looked like the sale racks at Bloomingdale's. There was a rail of suits, a stack of sweaters, boxes of belts, the wardrobes of certain designers, and a bottom shelf lined with shoes. I owned chaos. I used to open my closet and remember the lives those women led when I was wearing those clothes. A part of me became jealous of these women because they still lived with me and yet I led a different life from theirs. I imagined their lives in the closet. There was the one who was dressed for a Caribbean vacation, the corporate one who looked ready to create her own company, the sassy one off to a very cool party, and the quiet one who'd stay at home all day and read. They all lived in my closet. When I moved into the apartment I have now, I realized it was time to send them all on vacation. First I shipped the size eights off to my brother's house in Michigan, folded in boxes and cloaked in tissue. Then the size-ten box left for Michigan. The size twelves soon followed, and five years ago, I said farewell to the size fourteens. When my brother moved to a different house, I asked that he take my women with him. He refused, and I realized that I finally had to let them go. Everything that isn't me goes to help others, like the Dress for Success Worldwide organization. I am on the advisory board for New York. They provide women who have been out of work, due to hardship and heartbreak, with an outfit for a job interview. When they get the job, the organization gives each woman one more suit in order to start her new career. It feels wonderful to know that I am helping women dress for their new start in life.

Now it's time to release the women in your closet.

➤ TUNE IN

Look in your closet. Separate everything that is not your current size or that you feel no longer reflects who you are. Hopefully, you're beginning to learn this from the previous exercise. As you stand in front of the closet, ask yourself, What doesn't "belong" to me anymore? How will you know? In your journal, make an inventory of everything you have left.

➤ LIVE OUT LOUD

I'd like you to give away all the clothes that aren't you anymore. Take them to Goodwill shops, consignment stores, or charity organizations. Find charities in your area by looking in the Yellow Pages. Give yourself freedom at last in the knowledge that you've refined your style, and help someone find theirs. What's not right for you may be perfect for someone else. It's so liberating to feel that you have a closet that fully reflects who you are in the body you have today. You are living in the present, free from shadows and reminders of a former self. I'm proud of you, as others will be in the light of your generosity and compassion. Once you've given away the clothes that aren't a true reflection of you, let's play with your choices.

LEARNING CURVE 18

DRESS FOR *YOUR* SUCCESS

It's time to get dressed. Before we take in the whole picture, I want to dispel any of the negative beliefs you may be feeling with regard to clothes. First, there's the "I'm big, so why should I bother?" argument. Yes, you are a woman with curves. Showing a lack of interest in looking your best means that you're not embracing who you are today and celebrating your shape and style. Okay, you say, I am interested in clothes, but there's no choice for me. Oh, so you are interested? Good.

Well, I can tell you that there are more choices than ever for getting dressed as a full-figured woman. When I started working in the fashion industry, there were only two hundred companies making clothes for us. Today, there are over two thousand designers creating clothes for us. The choices for whichever shape you are and style you have exist in stores today. Okay, you say, you're telling me there are greater choices of sizes and styles just for me, but I don't like shopping. Sales assistants look down their noses at me. Tough one. All I can tell you is that sales assistants are paid to help you. Often they make a commission from your purchases. If you feel that you aren't being treated with respect, find someone who'll be only too willing to help find what you're looking for. Remember, *you* carry the wallet, so don't part with your hard-earned money if you feel that you haven't received the service you deserve.

And, finally, please enjoy the shopping experience, whether on the Internet, through a catalog, or in a store. It's fun, creative, and provides the opportunity for you to express who you are through clothes. You are as beautiful and worthy as everyone else. You always look good on the outside when you're feeling good on the inside.

You are the sum of your parts. Your thoughts, feelings, experiences, and tastes all make you who you are. In Step 3, I asked you to acknowledge the parts of your body you love and to begin to make peace with the parts that cause arguments. I'd be kidding myself if I thought that you would have accomplished this step by the time you've reached this chapter. Like certain aspects of your personality, there will always be parts of your body you want to play up and others you prefer to play down. This step will help you refine your style. Dressing with style is all about showing your assets and finding a way to play down those parts that you consider are not assets.

AUDREY'S STORY

Even as I talk to you right now, I feel good. If only you could see me. I'm wearing no bra, honey. You should see my breasts. I play them up whenever I can. I've always done so. In 1977, the Italian fashion house Fendi threw a party on their fabulous estate in Rome. It was the estate of life! My friend Eunice was with me. She asked me what I was going to wear. I said, "I don't know."

Honey, I knew *exactly* what I was going to wear! It was a Koos Van den Akker cotton two-piece with crisscross straps under the bust. When Eunice saw me in the hotel foyer in my dress, she said that she had to go back upstairs and change her clothes. She was so mad at me because I looked so good!

Truly, I think I have the most beautiful breasts. So I look for bras with no seams or underwires so people won't think I'm wearing a bra. V-necked tops best show off my cleavage. And I also have great legs. Basketball player's legs! I raise the hemline on my skirts, but I make sure they're not too short. Donna Karan makes the best panty hose. There's one that matches the color of my skin tone. I love that. If I choose to look sexy, I wear panty hose with seams. *Rrrrrrr.* The only part I play down is my stomach. I wear a fitted tunic that I don't tuck in and call it a day.

YVETTE'S STORY

If I want people to notice my body, color is how I do it. I'm usually an earth-tone lady, but when I want to look sassy, I go for red. That's when I think I'm hot stuff! I play up my breasts in dresses with a plunging neckline. And—boom!—people notice. I play down my waist by choosing not to wear anything tight around my waist. I don't feel comfortable. I can't stand being cinched in. Whenever I try to wear anything tight around my waist, I feel like I'm wearing a straitjacket. I like to feel comfortable, and I only feel great when I play up my bust and play down my waist.

MY STORY

I love my legs, my hands and feet, my face, and have a newly found love for my arms, so I highlight those areas when I get dressed. I play them up. I wear skirts with slits, sleeveless shells, and keep my fingernails and toes painted. I still have an argument with my stomach, so I've learned how to play that down. I'll wear a less fitted top, but team it up with a more fitted skirt to balance the proportion. If I want to accentuate my bust, I wear a shirt that's less buttoned on top. My makeup is natural and I frame my face with a pair of simple earrings. My smile is the thing I play up most. My whole face looks best when it's smiling. And that doesn't cost me a penny.

Dressing with style is not about dictates. But I have found that there are useful guidelines which help me to play up and play down certain features. Remember, these are just guidelines. Experiment with making the most of yourself. Here are some options.

	PLAYING IT UP	**PLAYING IT DOWN**
SHOULDERS	strapless dresses	structured jackets
	boat-necked tops	cardigan sweaters
	shells and tank tops	crew or V necks
NECK	turtleneck sweaters	jewel-necked tops
	funnel-necked tops	open-necked shirts
BUST	V-necked tops	crew-necked tops
	lower necklines	higher necklines
	knit tops	minimizing bras
	bustiers	tunic tops in darker colors
WAIST	belts and sashes	longer tunics
	blouses tucked in	men's shirts worn
	fitted tops	out
	circle skirts	A-line skirts
HIPS	knit skirts	A-line skirts
	slim flat-front pants	long skirts
	bias-cut skirts	dark colors
	narrow skirts	
LEGS	shorter skirts	fuller-leg trousers
	slits on skirts and	longer-length skirts
	dresses	and dresses
	pinstripes on pants	opaque stockings
	and skirts	
	capris	
	nude stockings	

ACCENTUATE THE POSITIVE

Tune in to playing up and dressing down.

> ➤ **TUNE IN**

In your Learning Curves journal, write a list of all the assets you want to emphasize. Ask yourself, Do I love my neck, shoulders, bustline, arms, waist, hips, legs, feet? Now make a list of all the areas you would prefer to play down.

> ➤ **LIVE OUT LOUD**

Before you make your next clothing purchase and for every purchase you make from now on, I'd like you to ask these two questions before you make your way to the checkout line:

1. Does this reflect my personal style?
2. Does this purchase play up the parts I love the most and downplay the ones I don't?

Answer these two questions before you hand over your money, and you'll never make another fashion faux pas or leave the clothing item forgotten in your closet. If you're not sure, leave it in the store and have the courage to walk out without it. It will be there tomorrow, and if not, someone else bought it to reflect her true style. There will be another opportunity for you to buy a more perfect reflection of you. The courage to say yes or no to something gives you the power to determine your style.

Always remember to play up what you love and downplay what you don't . . . yet.

Just checking. We don't look good in everything, because not every piece of clothing enhances what we want it to. The trick is to try all the styles and shapes available to us (and there are many), and if a piece of clothing doesn't achieve the effect we want to create, there will be that perfect piece that does. You'll know when it does, because you'll feel great in it. Now that you've begun to assess what parts of your body you want to play up and play down, we can begin to build your wardrobe.

YOUR LIFESTYLE WARDROBE NEEDS A SOLID FOUNDATION

Armed with your emerging style, your cleared-out closet, and your "I have to play that up and play that down" list, let's begin to build the wardrobe that reflects who you are. No matter what your taste or job (unless you work in a profession that requires you to wear a uniform), there are certain pieces that form the basis of any lifestyle wardrobe. It's a lesson I learned many years ago.

MY STORY

After clearing my closet of all the sizes and styles that no longer reflected my style, I was left with seven basic shapes or styles. That's right, my friend, seven silhouettes remained hanging in my closet. They were single-breasted jackets, white cotton shirts, narrow-cut pants, twinsets, one black dress, straight skirts with slits, and matte jersey tops and skirts. That's all. These items would form the cornerstones of the wardrobe for my present working life. Before then, I had hundreds of various-shaped jackets, dozens of different-shaped skirts, and more fabric in my closet than I knew what to do with. But no more. The theater days were gone. I was left to rebuild my wardrobe around the life I'd built for myself in the fashion industry. I'd wear the jacket over the dress for TV, put the twin-set over my skirt for attending a photo shoot, and wear the black dress from day to evening, with a change of accessory. Those items were what I needed to reflect my work, mood, personality, lifestyle, and sense of self.

From there, I began to expand my wardrobe, piece by piece. Each season, I added a color twinset to the basic colors I owned. In addition to my basic white shirt, I added gray and black shirts. And with each purchase, I have formed a wardrobe in which each piece works together with another piece. They interact. I now mix and match the pieces in my closet so that I can change the look while keeping my style. If you see an item you love and feel great wearing, consider buying it in more than one color. By doing so, you'll add items of clothing to your closet, thus enabling you to change your look but remain true to your style.

AUDREY'S STORY

In the small closet that I own now, I know each and every one of my pieces. My apartment is also my office: I work from home. As you know, my style is taken from men's dress. I still buy Craig Tailor shirts, which wash and iron like a dream. That's the style I like. If I want a pair of jeans, I get Levi's jeans to order. They come in every color, I love the fit, and they make them with a thirty-six-and-a-half-inch inseam. They're made for me! My shoes are mostly loafers. Again, I have Helene Arpels loafers in almost every color; they last forever, they're the right styling, and I've had them for fifteen years. And when it comes to sweaters: cashmere, cashmere, cashmere. None of that other stuff—it itches. Every woman over thirty-five should have one piece of cashmere in her closet. When I go on vacation, I take what I need in order to do what I need to do. The extras always come with the accessories. Whether it's an eighteen-karat gold coin necklace, a thirty-nine-dollar Diamonique ring, or a pair of leopard-print mules, I change the look according to how I want to feel. All the pieces in my wardrobe can be mixed and matched. For every top, I buy three bottoms. Remember, my father taught me that the pants always wear out first. Let me tell you something else: We don't all have the same amount of money, carry the same weight, or have the same color hair. But there's one thing we all have in common: twenty-four hours. What are you doin' with yours? I'm not spending mine figuring out what to wear with what. It's organized. I'm organized. My closet has everything I need. It expresses who I am. I know it like I know myself.

Building your closet with the pieces that reflect how you've built your life gives you the freedom to dress as you are. Dress without stress. Yes, we all have twenty-four hours in a day. There aren't a million days, so you don't need a million outfits. It's the power to mix and match suits as well as pieces in your closet that enables you to refine your style.

YVETTE'S STORY

After I cleared my closet, I could actually see through to the wooden back of it for the first time in ages. I found that I could fill in the spaces and gaps with the style I now owned. I add pieces to my closet each season, one of which is a "good piece": a made-to-measure suit. My mother always said that I should look for well-made, quality clothes. "Buy one good piece," she told me, "and it'll last you years." My mother was right. There are clothes I bought years ago and they still look great today. More important, I feel great in them.

Now that you've made room in your closet, your essential pieces will give you the power and the freedom to dress according to your own style. Keep asking yourself, What pieces best express who I am, and how can I team each piece with something I already own that's a true reflection of my style? Inspire yourself with new colors and inventive ways of marrying a skirt with a top. Magazines are great for ideas. They clue you in on the season's fashion trends and, for some magazines, what's available in the stores. But remember, it's you who chooses what you'll wear. Weave a wardrobe that makes your life easier.

Again, here are the seven pieces that enabled me to build a practical lifestyle wardrobe.

THE SEVEN PIECES

1. SINGLE-BREASTED JACKET

A single-breasted jacket has less fabric than a double-breasted one, so it won't gather awkwardly or make you look boxy. You can always ask for shoulder pads to be removed if you are broad-shouldered. Many jackets now come with detachable shoulder pads.

2. WHITE COTTON SHIRT

A white cotton shirt is transseasonal and always looks classically casual with a pair of jeans or with a skirt.

3. TAILORED PANTS

Narrow-leg pants always give the illusion of height. Pants without pleats—termed *flat-front pants*—also give a smoother line at the waist.

4. TWINSET

A twinset can be worn together or separately. They look as good with skirts as they do with pants and dresses. I like the cardigan worn as a top underneath a jacket.

5. DRESS

A solid-color dress in a neutral color—black, navy, brown, or beige—takes you from day to night. My suggestion would be to look for one first in a simple shift shape either fitted or straight. Look for whichever length you feel plays to your strengths.

6. STRAIGHT SKIRT

Everyone needs this classic knee-length skirt in their closet because it works well with a jacket or by itself with anything on top.

7. MATTE JERSEY TOPS AND SKIRTS

Last but not least, tops in matte jersey have stretch in them, so the fabric will hug your curves without clinging to them. If you prefer, try a long skirt or pants in the same fabric.

Now tune in to building your wardrobe.

➤ TUNE IN

No doubt you already have many of these pieces in your closet, but I know you're asking, How do I know they're the right ones? Building your wardrobe doesn't necessarily have to start with a shopping spree. You've already edited your closet down to the clothes that reflect your style. Look at what's left.

take these steps:

1. Do you have one of each of these items? The real test is to see whether each of the pieces remaining in your closet can work with the others. No piece can be considered a building block of your wardrobe unless you can wear it with several of your other pieces.

2. Can you take your favorite tops and wear them with the pants or skirts?

3. Does the jacket look good with both bottoms?

4. Could you wear the jacket with your jeans on the weekend or for casual Fridays with khakis at work?

5. Does the dress work with the cardigan? Try tying the cardigan around your neck as an accent with the dress.

6. Does the knit sweater from the twinset work under the jacket and with the skirts or pants?

7. Does the matte jersey top go with your pants or your skirt?

If anything left in your wardrobe doesn't meet this criteria, it is at best something you can reserve for occasional use, or it's quite possibly something you may need to let go of.

When you've gone through the process of seeing what you have and whether your pieces can be worn interchangeably, you will be left with a foundation for your wardrobe or a small shopping list of items to complete it.

➤ LIVE OUT LOUD

Armed with your shopping list, it's time to fill in the gaps. Shopping can be a daunting task. We often feel pressured by the urge to spend on the spot, without considering what we feel we really need. When I'm looking for specific things for my working wardrobe, I always consider other purchases off-limits. It helps me focus and minimizes the risk of coming home with more women who'll stay in the closet.

1. Play detective. Once you've targeted the item you need, investigate all the choices available to you. If you feel you need a jacket, for example, it's helpful to test-run as many styles as possible.

2. Ask yourself two questions: How does it feel? How do *I* feel? Remember, each designer cuts differently. When you feel you've found the perfect jacket, it's always good to ask the store what their return policy is. Many stores won't give you the cash back, but you can usually exchange an item within a given number of days.

3. Consider how varied the store's selection is.

4. If you feel you've made a mistake when you've gotten something home, it's not a good idea to toss it in the closet and cut the tags off.

5. Always keep your receipt.

Once you find the basic pieces, how do you build from here? My advice is this. When you have identified what shapes you look and feel best in, you have a point of reference from which you can vary the look without changing your style. For example, if you like the way a straight skirt looks on you, try finding the same shape but in a different fabric or with a different detail. A skirt with a side or back slit provides two choices. Similarly, lighter wool or cotton is great for summer; heavier wool or bouclé will serve you well in winter.

If you'd like to introduce color for a season, think about choosing a top in a certain color that you can wear under your jacket or over your pants. Remember, whole outfits in bright orange are less versatile, less corporate, and more expensive

HOW THE SEVEN PIECES WORK

than buying one piece in that color. Subtle accents will allow you to keep updating your wardrobe. These trendier pieces need not be expensive. Like a carton of milk, they have a shelf life. So you don't need to overspend on them.

TAILORED CLOTHES AFFIRM YOUR UNIQUENESS

When you feel you've bought your perfect jacket or pants, there's one thing I'd like you to do before you wear it to a job interview that is coming up or to the office. Make sure it fits. As I've said before, full-figured women are not all one size. Just as we are unique individuals, we also have uniquely individual bodies.

Although the world labels us a size, that number doesn't reflect the shape of our curves. Making clothes fit *you* gives you a finished look. If you want to look like a professional in a corporate environment, it's important to dress like one. There's nothing that makes me feel better than finding an outfit that's totally me and having it fit perfectly for my curves. Just as you are tailor-made, your clothes look best when they are tailored for *you*.

AUDREY'S STORY

As you know, when I was a child, my clothes were made specially for me every Easter and Palm Sunday. Today, I still take my clothes to the tailor. I go the Ralph Lauren men's Polo shop at Saks Fifth Avenue, find my blazer, and then go upstairs to have it altered in the waist, shoulders, and sleeves. I have it altered at no extra charge, and honey,

"Miss Thing" has the perfect blazer. I remember buying something once in the women's department, and they wanted to charge me for alterations. I said that I wanted to speak to the manager. Curtly, the sales assistant asked me my name. "I am Audrey Smaltz!" I said. Bemused, the assistant beckoned the manager. I remarked to her that men didn't have to pay for their alterations, so why should we? After a few minutes of acting flustered, she agreed that I shouldn't have to pay, either. So, remember, if stores want to charge you for alterations, tell them that men aren't told they have to pay.

YVETTE'S STORY

After choosing something that reflects my personal style, I take it straight to the tailor. When clothes are bought off the rack, the shape is cut from a standard pattern, which doesn't account for where *my* curves are. I appreciate that I am unique, and having my clothes tailored to fit *me* is just another great thing I do for myself. It makes me feel special. As I mentioned before, I can't stand wearing anything tight around my waist. Even my tailored clothes aren't altered so that they're tight. Like having a manicure or pedicure, tailored clothes make me respect my body and enable me to look and feel my best.

If for any reason you can't find what you're looking for in a store, consider having it made. I do. Sewing is a great way to create what you want. I think it's so important to have choices that I have developed a series of Learning Curves Patterns for Butterick. If you can't sew yourself, have a tailor make something for you. Not only do I show my tailor patterns I want made up, but often I will show him a skirt I already own, and he duplicates the style in the fabric I want. Remember, having a simple skirt made in a style you love is a great way of updating your style. And sometimes it's less expensive than buying off the rack.

➤ TUNE IN

Think about what clothes you need to have altered in order for your closet to fit into your life. I want you to confide in the mirror. I have three mirrors in my apartment. One for my face, one for my midsection, and the full-length mirror in my bedroom. Look at the whole package from head to toe.

now ask yourself:

1. Do I feel good?
2. Do the clothes feel good on my body?
3. Do I like the way they fit?
4. Do I need to have them altered?

➤ LIVE OUT LOUD

Here are a few guidelines I feel you should follow before having your clothes tailored.

1. Excess fabric adds bulk. Often, we buy a jacket in a larger size so that it will feel more comfortable. When it's larger, it's larger all over, not just in the places we're trying to conceal. This usually isn't problematic for soft pieces like sweaters and blouses, but tailored pieces look best when they are tailored for you.

2. When you buy a jacket in a larger size to accommodate a fuller bust or larger stomach, the shoulders are often too big for you. The shoulder seam on the jacket should be perfectly aligned to where your shoulder and arm connect. Once you have it tailored this way, the jacket will fit *your* body and it won't leave you looking boxy. Who wants to look like a refrigerator?

3. Always bear in mind that any horizontal line, be it the hem of a jacket or the bottom of a blouse, is a focal point and creates width. To avoid making yourself look wider in places you'd rather not, make sure that the horizontal lines cross your body in areas that you're less concerned

about. For example, every time I buy a jacket, I stand in the three-way mirror to ensure that the jacket hits me in the right place. I ask my tailor to raise and lower the jacket hem until we find the place that it's the most flattering. I've found that jacket hems that fall below my rear are the most flattering for me.

4. If you'd like to play up your waist, ask your tailor to nip in the waist of your jacket or coat.

5. Sleeve lengths are a big topic of debate. A classic length that is flattering for most women is a sleeve that falls at the wristbone.

6. The most flattering pant length is usually one that falls to the top of the heel of your shoe. If you know which shoes you will wear most often with the pair of pants you're having altered, take them to the tailor with you.

7. The issue of skirt length is less about any hard-and-fast tips I can give you and more about the relationship you have with your legs. Some of us love our legs and others are less enamored. My suggestion is for you to wear the skirt length you feel best with. I love my legs but choose not to wear a very short skirt. I show them off by wearing skirts with slits or narrow skirts that fall just below the knee, and, yes, I'm a sucker for a pair of high heels. If your legs aren't your favorite body part, have the tailor keep your skirts on the longer side and best avoid high slits.

8. Remember to check and see what you need done when you are at the store. Often, a store's policy is that unfinished trouser hems and jacket sleeves can be shortened free of charge.

Always choose what you feel looks best on you, the clothes that allow you to shine. Like telling a story, it's the structure that provides order and allows for your expression to flow. Organizing your closet enables you to be creative within your style. Now that you've looked at the basics, it's time to spread your wings.

Stretching Your Style

We've been told and believed that us girls shouldn't wear this and that. I've never paid much attention to what was in fashion. There are choices for all of us. Be proud of who you are. It's a mind-set. Show your body instead of trying to hide it.

DELTA BURKE, ACTOR AND DESIGNER

BREAK THE FASHION RULES AND CREATE YOUR OWN

It's time to break a few rules. No, not the ones that will land you in jail, but, rather, the fashion rules we've been told that we *had* to follow. First of all, what are the "no big girl can wear that" rules? Stripes across the body, florals, bright colors, and fitted clothes have been handed down to us as the no-nos of full-figured dressing. Many of us have spent our lives apologizing for the way we are and so we've felt that blending in with a crowd will make us less visible if we wear dark colors and boxy shapes. Hiding your style is self-censorship. As you know, fashion follows the crowd, but style makes your true self stand out.

The fashion industry often forgets that a size eighteen wants what a size eight wants. Buyers, the people who select each collection for the stores before the season begins, sometimes err on the side of caution when they choose what you will wear each season. So, instead of letting us dare to try something different, we've been told season after season that "boxy and with major shoulder pads" or "loose and flowing" are still "in fashion" for us. Yawn. It's like having your mother choosing your party dress when you're five years old. You want to wear the pretty pink one with all the ribbons and lace, but your mother's already chosen the "safe" navy swing dress that buttons to the neck. Moreover, you *feel* like a frump in the dull navy dress. How you feel is how you look.

The good news is that full-figured clothes are now giving us more choice. More choice means more freedom. More freedom means more fun. More fun means that you can stretch your style and, yes, you have the opportunity to develop a signature that's uniquely you. Give yourself the permission to try on something that has your personality sewn into the lining.

All women would prefer to accentuate certain body parts and play down others. But that doesn't mean you can't experiment with the parts you love while remaining true to your style. It's important that when your eye gravitates to a color or print, you take it for a test run first. Take it into the fitting room, try it on, and see how you look. How do *you* feel in it? Ignore the old rules, because *they* simply don't fit. Sooner or later, all myths are shattered: Women can't vote, most women can't be funny, professional women can't be CEOs, doctors, or judges, and blond women can't be smart. And full-figured women can't be stylish? Well, we can. We just need to give ourselves a break. That's our opportunity to break the rules.

Anna Scholz is a plus-size German fashion designer who lives in London, England. She walked into my life three years ago at the first Lane Bryant fashion show I ever attended. She's a six-feet-one blond bombshell with an explosive personality. She loves her body and dresses with major attitude. We giggle when we're out for dinner, and she shares my continued desire to push fashion beyond the limitations of size. The clothes she designs are fabulous, and I am proud to own a few of them. She's a woman who uses her craft to break the rules.

ANNA'S STORY

I never felt the fashion rules applied to me. Although my parents told me that I couldn't wear this and that, that I couldn't be too loud because I was bigger and I couldn't make a statement, I just thought, Sod it! Germany, the country where I grew up, is terribly conservative. I guess my parents were buying into someone else's rules about how I should look. I didn't blend in. At six-one and a size eighteen by the time I was sixteen, I promised myself that I wouldn't hide anymore. I'd stop apologizing for the way I was and I'd only try to make a positive statement about myself. It was then that I truly began to like myself. Love myself. My philosophy is the same as it was at sixteen. It is that I'd rather be liked by some than ignored by all. At sixteen years old, I made myself an orange dress with lots of plastic yellow flowers sewn onto it. I'd wear it with vintage cowhide platform shoes and walk around the streets of Hamburg wearing my personality. Wearing *my* style. I felt so free.

I moved to London in my early twenties to study at the famous Central Saint Martins, arguably the best art and fashion college in Europe. But there was one problem. No one at the college was particularly interested in plus-size clothes. The college had no pattern blocks for plus sizes or any plus-size mannequins. So, I went to the flea market on London's Portobello Road and bought an old mannequin with screws that expanded the torso. Perfect. I carried it into college and started designing my collection of full-figured clothes. I presented the collection on six different women, all with very different curves, which took a lot of time because each outfit had to be handmade and individually tailored. I finished the same year as Paul McCartney's daughter Stella. While she had her supermodel friends Kate Moss and Naomi Campbell model her clothes, I had six beautiful, real women model mine. The press loved it.

Now, as a full-figured designer of full-figured clothes and someone who loves to break the rules, I say to my customers that I make clothes to fit women and I don't feel that women should change their bodies in order to fit the clothes.

As full-figured women, we need to think outside the box in creating our own styles. We owe it to ourselves to strive for a unique style because the fashion industry won't do it for us. To conform is to compromise. We don't have to settle for anything less than we deserve or desire. There is little point in breaking rules just for the sake of breaking them. But always be open to the truth that your inner gifts can be presented on the body you own.

Delta Burke is one of the most beautiful women on television. Famous for her role as Suzanne Sugarbaker in *Designing Women,* she overcame the producers' size prejudice, married actor Gerald McRaney, a wonderful man who loves her for who she is, and now is creating her own clothing empire: Delta Burke Design. Delta and I met for the first time when we were both guests on *Oprah.* I found her to be gracious, smart, strong, and someone who owns her femininity. She's a woman I truly admire.

DELTA'S STORY

Once I dealt with who I was and the difference in me, I felt comfortable being myself. While at school in London [what is it about London?], I discovered my dramatic style. I came back to America wearing nothing but black: big black hats with veils, cloaks, and walking sticks with a sword inside them. Fascinated by early Hollywood, my first apartment was filled with posters of Vivien Leigh and Marilyn Monroe. Forties-style clothes looked really good on me. And I felt great in them. But after moving to Hollywood, I realized that the casting directors and producers didn't know what to make of me. I didn't look like a California girl and didn't wear that casual California elegance. I didn't conform. I didn't want to.

I showed up for auditions in a forties-style suit, seamed stockings, and my hair in a snood, and they loved the look. I loved costume drama and I wanted to celebrate the female form. In 1994–95 I did a series called *Women of the House.* The press said that I shouldn't wear fitted clothes and that color would make me look fatter. I thought, why should I try to be something I'm not? I'm big. Get over it. I can either be big and dumpy in a

When you dress as you are and not according to an outdated set of beliefs, you can experience the joy of knowing yourself. You choose what you like and what you don't, what feels good and what best expresses who you are. The world is full of laws and rules. Style makes one request: Listen to your heart. We break rules every day; the corporate promotion in an all-male environment, becoming a working mother, marrying the person we love even though our parents don't approve, or deciding against the odds to go back to school. Stretching your style gives you that chance to break free from whatever rules have been set. Break the rules and set your own.

Like me, Nikki Bordeaux is another midwesterner who had many careers before choosing to work in the fashion-publishing industry. I feel that if I were to have an alter ego, I would choose this sensitive, effusive young woman who looks to her future with wide-eyed enthusiasm.

NIKKI'S STORY

The biggest rule that I have broken is not always to wear black. I try not to wear black every day. I like the quirkiness of clothes and I like certain colors and the feel of fabric against my skin. I never believed I should cover myself up. I've always been comfortable in my skin. My mother grew up in an abusive household and no one ever told her that she was beautiful. When she became a mother, she knew that she was never going to deny me that. She always made me feel that I was beautiful. In fact, my stepfather told her to stop telling me I was beautiful because I would believe it. She answered him that she hoped I did. Although my mother liked to buy me neutral colors and classic styles, I found that I was drawn to color and separates.

I've always been inspired by people on the street. But I never copy somebody else. That's why I love vintage clothes. They help me express whatever part of my personality I want to show on any given day. I wear what feels right for me. I don't care about designer names or logos. My mom said that those things would just go out of fashion and I'd get tired of them. She was right. I buy things from vendors on the street, like Kangol caps. Only they're not Kangol! I'm constantly stretching my eclectic style by pushing against fashion dictates. I dare myself. I make myself look the way I want to look and feel. Above everything else, I just want to look cute.

MY STORY

My mother always told me that I shouldn't wear fitted clothes. But one day I broke the rule. I was fifteen years old and my mother owned a Diane von Furstenberg dress, printed in a geometric pattern of blues and rust against white. It was a wrap dress. Now, I was told never *ever* to wear belts to define my waist because, according to my mother, I had never had a waist. The dress broke every rule. It had stretch in it to hug my butt and had a deep V neck to give me great cleavage. It was so sexy. I borrowed it from her closet and wore it to a

Sweet Sixteen luncheon with a pair of strappy sandals. And I felt really sexy.

That day, I challenged the rule that my clothes have to be bigger and looser. I challenged the idea that sexiness comes in a certain package, one that's smaller or found only on the pages of a magazine. I realized that sexiness comes from inside. Once I gave myself the permission to stretch my style and push the boundaries, I found the freedom to challenge all the rules. I've been breaking the rules ever since. Now when I want to wear more fitted clothes, all I ask myself is, Who said I couldn't?

When it comes to breaking the old fashion rules, I have learned that there are ways to break them without breaking your heart or, for that matter, the bank. Let's identify the rules we've been told about the clothes we can't wear and I'll suggest some ways of wearing them.

COLOR WAYS

Use color creatively. Think about the colors in a flower shop, the roses in your garden, or the Crayola crayons that children use. Find *your* colors. You could go to town with color on your choice of accessories. I find that color on the body looks best when it's offset by darker colors. That means darker hosiery, a darker shoe, or a darker top underneath a brightly colored suit. You can also reverse that by taking your neutral navy or black suit, and pop it with a cobalt- or tangerine-colored top. This is an opportunity for you to play. I love unusual combinations like brown with lavender, camel and red, black and turquoise and navy with fuchsia. Forget about being a "summer" or "winter" person. Just experiment with colors you see and love.

THE WINDOW OF POSSIBILITIES

STRIPE ME DOWN

Stripes look especially great in knitwear. But there's one thing I urge you to think about: the direction of the stripes. Horizontals widen and verticals lengthen the body. You can avoid looking like you're wearing a tube of toothpaste by choosing finer lines. I always find that stripes are a great way of highlighting the parts I want to play up. For example, narrow horizontal lines across the bust play up cleavage and vertical stripes on pants call attention to the length of your legs. Now that I've said that stripes are great, we have to talk about shades. Shades are really important when delving into the graphic world. I suggest that you look for stripes that are in the same color range. That means that a darker sweater looks best with a darker stripe, like black and deep violet. Or choose a lighter-colored sweater with a lighter-colored stripe. For example, a white sweater with a khaki stripe. Having said that, let's break a rule. Black or navy and white stripes are so classic that they're always a good choice.

IN PRINT

Prints are a fashion conundrum. The fashion world has traditionally said no, no, no! to them—especially when it comes to girls with fuller figures. But I say that a little bit goes a long way. My preference is to choose a print, in geometric shapes, animal prints, or florals, where there's more of the solid background on the clothing item than on the print itself. I would have to say that oversize prints and big swirly flowers look better in a child's painting than on the body. But printed accessories? Go for it. Choose from bags, scarves, and even shoes. Just remember: A solid color on the body balances out the bold accessories.

THREE SHEERS

Sheer fabric is very sexy. Come on, this is all about the illusion of skin. If you're concerned about your arms or bust, think about this: sheer overlays on sleeves, around the neck, or over a skirt, suggesting merely a hint of sensuality. Try wearing sheer in a darker color, like black, navy, or burgundy. I love sheer for its subtle allure. When it's too sheer, consider layering. At *Mode* three years ago, I joined Sylvia Heisel for a "Designers Who Break Rules" story. I was photographed with her in the same sheer mint-colored tunic, layered over a pistachio-colored tunic, with mine over a turquoise silk column dress and hers over leggings. If you want to play safe, try a sheer blouse over a tank top. If you want to play daring, go for a black bra under an animal-print sheer shirt.

BEFITTING

Depending on your curves, clothes that gently form to your body are more flattering than loose shapes. I always wear the more fitted pieces on the parts I want to play up, such as a looser top and a more fitted bottom. This is because I think my legs are a great asset. Conversely, you may prefer a more fitted top with a looser bottom if you love your bust.

YOUR BATHING SUIT

Swimsuits look great in solid colors. Of course, there's the ever-popular understated, perfectly practical . . . black. I usually stay away from printed swimsuits. If prints are your cup of tea, I warn you to look for muted floral patterns and small dots with a dark background. It's the details that help to give us a broader choice. You may want to look for swimsuits that have bust support in underwire or built-in bras. Consider texture in the fabric, like metallic finishes and matte fabrics, athletic details like zippers, or color block to enhance your bustline. Look for interesting straps like spaghetti or braided widths and ones with metal detail. Always test-run first. And by all means, dare yourself to try a bikini if you feel confident wearing one. I highly suggest looking for one that covers your derriere.

Now I'd like you to tune in to breaking the rules.

➤ **TUNE IN**

In your Learning Curves journal, make a list of all the rules you've used to limit the way you dress. Call it your "I can't wear" list. When you have finished, I want you to ask yourself, Is it possible that these statements aren't true? If you answer yes, dare yourself to consider breaking the rules.

➤ **LIVE OUT LOUD**

Today, I'd like you to begin to take risks. Pick an old rule most opposed to your emerging style. For example, if you've always believed that full-figured women can't wear sexy clothes but you're realizing that your tastes are somewhat sexy, go try on a shorter skirt. How does it feel? If it feels right, go ahead and break another rule. Set your own rules.

In fashion at least, rules are there to be broken. Keep stretching your style, testing the waters, breaking down barriers, and trying something different so that you can have fun with your style. Nothing is set in stone. In fashion, there is an eleventh commandment: "Thou shalt break the rules." Think about what you'd love to try and never thought you could, and challenge yourself to step into the fitting room with a new piece of clothing and push yourself beyond your own boundaries.

SIGNATURE STYLE

Your Signature Says Something Uniquely You

When creating your own look, you inevitably create a signature. What is it that makes you special? What's the common thread running through your closet? Or could it be something you never take off and is distinctively you? Your signature is how people define you and it's a way of defining yourself. Think about this. When you're on vacation and you're buying a gift for a friend, what do you buy for them that you feel is characteristically them? What do friends buy you that makes them say, "I knew you'd love this"? Is it a bangle, because they always see you wearing stacked bangles on your wrist? Is it a leopard print, because your bedroom is done in that animal print? What's your signature?

Signatures are as powerful as word association. Recall a name, and a signature often comes to mind. When we think of Coco Chanel, we remember the camellia and strands of pearls she always wore. Camryn Manheim is recognized for her twelve ear piercings up her right ear. Jackie Onassis was known for her dark glasses. Talk-show host Sally Jessy Raphael is famous for her red-rimmed eyeglasses. Whatever your signature, people remember you for it. It's your special stamp of style. It's a characteristic you are known and appreciated for and it signifies your innate individuality. Sometimes your signature changes according to the way you feel, but it always remains a true reflection of your style.

ANNA'S STORY

My signature varies with each collection I design. My signature looks are colorfully feminine and sensual and I work within those moods to create my signature style. I show a lot of cleavage, since I feel that it's my best asset. So I'll wear a thin spaghetti-strap dress with a plunging neckline and feel great wearing it. I designed a black jacket with fringing over it, so when I move, the jacket sways around my curves.

My signature at the moment is colorful florals. I own several duster coats, each printed with colorful flowers, and I feel modern and feminine in them. On vacation in Milan, I lived in a hot-pink suit worn over a black T-shirt with the word *sexy* written in red rhinestones. I got so many compliments. Mostly, I feel my signature lies in the accessories I choose. Flowery hair clips are a favorite, and I have dozens. If a friend were to buy me a gift, that's what I'd be given.

DELTA'S STORY

I've never paid much attention to what's in fashion. As you know, my signature look is dramatic, but my signature piece has evolved. It used to be that any excuse I had to wear a corset would make me happy if it was for "dress-up." But when it became a necessity as I gained weight, I remember always feeling restricted in them. I felt uncomfortable in them and too aware of myself. So now I choose clothes that are still dramatic but don't bind me in any way. I have to say that above all else, my signature piece is a pair of black high-heeled boots. I still wear them with leggings. That's my look, my signature.

NIKKI'S STORY

I have a signature style as well as a signature piece. I've always worn a pair of gold hoop earrings. My mother gave them to me when I was in high school and I said I would never wear them. They've become my favorite piece of jewelry. They are part of me and I hardly ever take them off.

I now own a closet that reflects my signature style. Whatever I find in my room in the morning is what I will wear. I'm from the Midwest. And I have days when I can't believe I am living in New York City. I've always had fun—a lot of it. People always labeled me a New Yorker even though I'd never been to New York until I was a junior in college. What I'm saying is that I have a big-city attitude for a small-town girl. The signature of my style just grows. I look back at pictures of myself and remember how big I was on polka dots. My prom dress for junior high was a long, puckered polka-dot dress in black and white. It had a drop waist and a full skirt from the hip with a bow! I saw somebody wearing them the other day and I thought, Oh my God! I used to rock polka dots. The chance to speak to students as an editor made me see how very lucky I am to have a job that allows me to express and explore myself. It made those students all feel that they can discover themselves and that if you want to be somewhere, go there—even with your style.

Experimentation is the key to finding your signature. Remember, you may have a signature piece, like Nikki's earrings, as well as a signature style. Ask yourself, What do I want to say about myself? Question what you've been told you "can't" wear. Be open to the possibility that *your* way is the right way. Your signature is yours. Claim who you are through your choice of personal expression. Imitation may be the sincerest form of flattery, but originality is the truest form of style.

MY STORY

There are certain things I've worn forever: a watch, a ring, and a bracelet, all on my left hand. It's my trademark. The degrees have varied over the years, sometimes on different fingers, different widths, or more than one bracelet. But you'll always see them on me. Sometimes they get used in fashion shoots. Roseanne Barr took the ring off my hand during a fashion shoot with former clothing designer Isaac Mizrahi. Roseanne said, "I need the ring." I replied, "You can borrow the ring, but you can't have the ring." She said, "No, *I* want the ring!" And I responded with laughter: "Well that's too bad, because *the ring* is from Paris, and I'm not going back to Paris right now, so I get to keep the ring!" It was a *Seinfeld* moment. It was so funny to see my ring in the photograph, because it's very much a part of me. Seriously, though, for Roseanne to keep my ring would feel like taking a part of me. People even called me, saying, "That's *your* ring." I said to them, "I know—enough of the ring already!"

Your signature is like wearing your personality. It's a conversation piece. It catches the eye over a dinner date and your partner wants to know more about it. More about you. Today, I'd like you to think about what it is that you consider your signature.

WHAT'S YOUR BAG?

Tune in to your signature.

➤ **TUNE IN**

In your Learning Curves journal, cut out ideas from magazines and create a scrapbook. Include pictures of signature looks you are drawn to. Are you a style fan of Audrey Hepburn, Marilyn Monroe, Grace Kelly, or Eva Perón? Ask yourself, Am I an eye, scarf, color, shoe, or jewelry person? (Or all of the above!) What is my trademark? Is it something I've owned for years? Is it a variation on a theme I love? What feels like an extension of myself? If you don't already have a signature piece, make a list of the accessories that have caught your eye from the pictures you've collected.

➤ **LIVE OUT LOUD**

Have fun finding your signature. Experiment with a new eyeglasses frame, shoe heel, or jewelry metal, and when you're shopping, mention whose style inspires you. For example, say that you're looking for Jackie O–style sunglasses or a Duchess of Windsor panther-style pin. Now go out and find that extra piece of yourself.

Creating your signature gives you the opportunity to say something unique about yourself. It's the chance to be individual. Open yourself to the possibility that you can find a signature piece that expresses who you are: your humor, irony, and the wild aspect of your personality. There's a story in everything, and I ask you to bring your signature story to life. Wear it with style.

IT TAKES CONFIDENCE TO MAKE AN ENTRANCE

The outer style you have found, refined, and stretched now gives you confidence to make an entrance. What woman doesn't want to make an entrance? Who would rather look at the groom instead of the bride on your best friend's wedding day? Why is the prom such an *event*? Why are we glued to the television when the Oscars are shown live? Remember, this book is all about you: your life, your style, your opportunity to make heads turn and hearts open as the leading lady in your own life.

Self-confidence is within you. This is the moment to let it shine. Think of yourself, proud and beautiful. Confidence is charm. It attracts people to you, strangers and friends. If confidence were an object, it would effervesce like a soda and sparkle like champagne. Making an entrance gives you the opportunity to announce your style.

ANNA'S STORY

I love making an entrance. It's all about making an effort to dress as myself and feeling a strong sense of my power as a woman. I remember going to the nightclub Kinky Galinky some years ago. The crowd was really trendy. Queues of partygoers encircled the entrance to the club and the bouncers were strict about who would get in. I got out of the cab a few yards from the crowd, now thick with people waiting to party. I wore a fitted sheer black dress cut so low at the back that you could see the top part of my bottom through the sheer. Well, the club was called *Kinky* Galinky! Noticing one of the bouncers look at me as I arrived to join the crowd, I turned myself around and then faced him with a smile. Loudly, he urged the crowd, "Stand aside!" and I got in the club without waiting a moment. I felt so confident within myself that it immediately attracted the bouncer's eye.

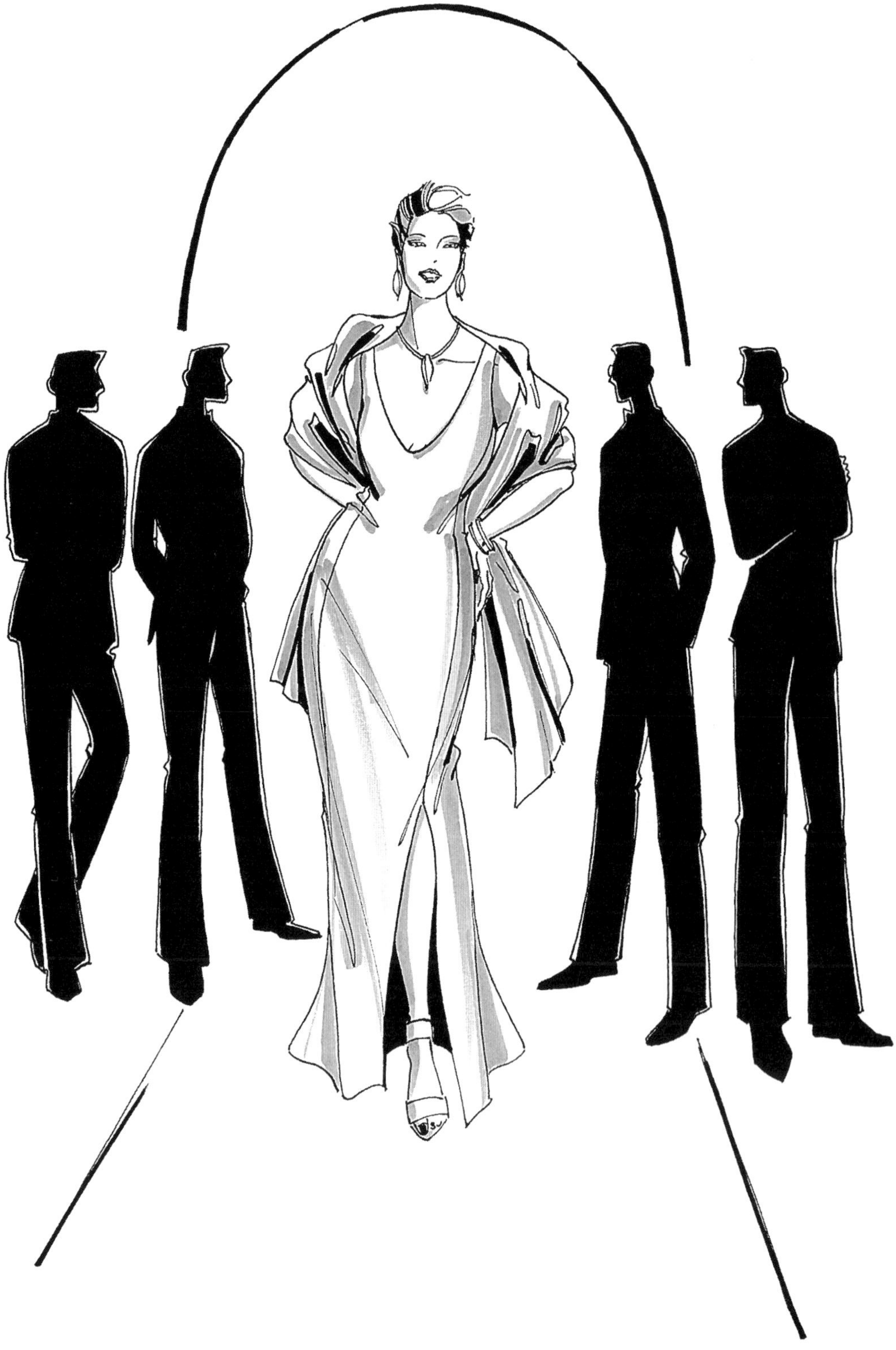

DELTA'S STORY

I had to go to a Hollywood function in my early days as an actress. With my fondness for drama, I found an evening gown that would make an entrance. It was a hot-pink sequined dress with a low-shaped back. Looking both scandalous and exciting, I couldn't wait to wow Hollywood in that dress. I arrived in the dress and I felt fabulous. The hot-pink color was very different from my signature black, but I still felt dramatic and sexy. It was still true to my style. And you know what? That night was the first time I walked out of a party and strangers were calling my name.

If you feel like the belle of the ball, you will not be mistaken for the pumpkin. Think about the effect you want to create. Remember your most magical entrance-making moments.

NIKKI'S STORY

Recently, I had to go to this magazine-world black-tie event. I chose to wear this beautiful bias-cut black V-necked velvet gown with my body slip under it. It was so perfect. I felt like a star when I walked into the party. Everyone just turned around and said, "Nikki?" I know everyone thought I looked fabulous that night because I felt so good.

I feel like I make an entrance outside of the dressy fashion events I've been to. What I think gets people to notice me is my smile. I love that my happiness makes other people happy. People are always waiting for me to arrive at a party because I enjoy the time I have so much that they get happy, too. Happiness is contagious. I've known people have enjoyed my company since I was six years old. When you feel that people enjoy being with you, you have the confidence to do anything simply by being yourself.

The confidence to make an entrance is also fueled by the feeling that people want to be with you while you're at that party. If you're having fun, others have fun around you. Have a great time. Entrances can be loud or quiet, but the level of confidence you have always depends on feeling good about who you are and observing the way others feel around you.

MY STORY

I adore getting dressed for events. I'm always late because I like to make an entrance. I love the luxury of taking a long bubble bath and pampering myself. It's the time I spend with myself, and, as we all know, the preparation is as much fun (if not more so) as the event itself. I have a favorite entrance-making moment. It was a Spring Gala Dance at the Metropolitan Museum of Art in New York. The main party was in the Temple of Dendur. I wore a Carolina Herrera taupe-gold Greek goddess dress. The long dress wrapped underneath the bust, was piped in matte gold around the cuffs, and had a very high slit up the back. I wore it with gorgeous sandals and glittery hosiery. From the lingerie to the hosiery to the outside, everything made me feel fabulous.

My date, Jared, escorted me. There he was in his tuxedo, and he smiled with delight when he saw me. We arrived for the party in the conservatory-like space. The moonlight poured in from the glass roof. I knew people were staring at me and many paid me compliments. It's truly a magical evening when you appreciate the way you look and others appreciate it as they share the moment with you.

MAKING AN ENTRANCE

Black tie provides a great opportunity for us to make an entrance. As the dress code stipulates, dressing up to the nines is what's required. Pressure comes from feeling that everyone will be looking at what you're wearing. And they most probably will be. Add to the pressure the fact that most of us aren't used to dressing up on a regular basis. Here's how you can take the stress out of a formal affair.

1. Preparation is key.
2. Several weeks before the event, spend an afternoon looking to see what's in the stores.
3. When making your choices keep a few things in mind: First, you don't have to opt for something black and sequined to meet the dress code. I choose to wear separates for day and also do the same for evening, such as a long black skirt with a knit shell and satin jacket. But if a more formal approach to dressing up appeals to you, go for it.
4. Ask if you can take the clothes home to try on and what the store policy is if you decide to return them. It's important to give your new evening outfit a test run around the bedroom before you decide to keep it.

5. Make sure that you are comfortable in it. Are you going to be fussing with the shoulder strap all night or concerned that you are going to fall out of your bustier? No matter how good you look in it, if you are not comfortable, you won't have a good time.

6. For special-occasion clothes, there may be a greater need to have them altered to fit you. Give yourself plenty of time. If the alterations take longer for any reason, you won't need to feel the added pressure that the outfit won't be ready in time.

7. When you think you've found the ideal ensemble, ask yourself, Will I wear it again after this event? If so, you've probably picked a good investment.

8. You may want to look for an inexpensive satin evening bag if all you own are day bags.

9. Look for a pair of dressy shoes that you can wear time and again to other such functions and that perfectly complement the clothes you'll wear that night. Sandals, pumps, heeled mules, and slingbacks in satin are the most versatile.

Tune in to making a confident entrance.

➤ TUNE IN

Imagine yourself walking into a room. Picture it vividly in your head. Perhaps you have a function or party to go to in a couple of weeks. Imagine the experience.

In your Learning Curves journal, write down:

1. The outfit you'll wear

2. The hairdo you'll try

3. The entrance you'll make

4. The conversations you'll have

5. How you'll feel

➤ LIVE OUT LOUD

As you're getting ready for the event, replay the scene in your head. Rehearse confidently walking through the door, looking radiant and beautiful. See the positive response you get from the people in the room. Feel how calm, confident, and self-assured you are. Just breathe. Now, go and make that entrance.

Step 7

Dating with Style

If you put out, 'I'm a fat person, nobody likes me, I wish I had a date,' that's what you get back. If, on the other hand, you put out, 'I think I'm kind of beautiful, I like what I look like, and I have a lot to offer the world,' that's how people will respond to you.

KATHY NAJIMY, ACTOR

FEELING DESIRABLE IS THE KEY TO BEING DESIRED

According to 6,000 women's responses to an orgasm survey by *Weight Watchers* magazine (August 1995), three-fourths said that their sex partners find them attractive at their present weight. And that's not all. A full 85 percent said they "always" or "usually" enjoy sex. Only 10 percent said they "never" enjoy sex. But wait, it gets better: 70 percent of fuller-figured women said they almost always have orgasms, compared to just 29 percent of thin women. I'm not one for competition, especially between women; I really believe we all should stick together. But when I first saw these figures, I couldn't help letting my imagination run away with me. I envisioned the Orgasm Olympics, where big *beat* thin in the dizzying competition to reach new heights of sexual satisfaction. Thinner women may be on the covers of magazines and have a greater selection of clothes to buy, but in this arena at least, it's bigger women who come out on top. Go for the gold. But the rewards aren't just physical. They include romance, companionship, and love. You, too, can have all this. It all starts with a feeling; feeling desirable.

What makes you feel desirable? What's your attraction? Think about the first time you realized your power as a woman. The very first time I discovered my effect on guys, I was twelve and was sitting on a beanbag with my friend Eric. We were chatting. I got up for a moment to adjust my position, and I ended up sitting on him. His breathing deepened and his legs stiffened. I thought I was squashing him. So I said to him, "Shall I get up?" He replied, "No." He was enjoying it. I could feel it. I had this effect as a girl. Not a big girl—just a girl. This is the power we have. Remember that. You are woman first. You have that. Own it.

Many things make us feel attractive: clothes, beauty treatments, someone else's interest in us, and people's compliments. They are, to use the fashion term, accessories. And yes, they are all important in helping us feel good. But our attractiveness is first found inside of us. What makes you attractive is measured by how well you think of yourself, not by how pretty your dress looks. I'd be lying if I said looks aren't important at all. But it's *your* look and *your* style that make people want to be with you.

Kathy Najimy is the funniest woman around. Now as I watch Kathy on the TV sitcom *Veronica's Closet,* I see the most striking woman. She is in love with her life, her husband, and her child. Here's a woman who inhabits the world with humor and strength, bluntness and integrity.

KATHY'S STORY

I have always *not* acted like how people think a fat person is supposed to act. I have never been one to sit on the couch and grab a pillow to hide my body. I've never *not* danced. I've never dressed in big, loose clothes. I try to carry myself in a way that says "whatever"—I don't necessarily care what you think: this is *my* body. I've spent several years learning how to step into my skin and show the world whatever "bright light" or great gifts I have to offer. And when you get to that point, you almost always get back the same gifts and respect. Once you let go of the stigma, people treat you with a different kind of regard. I'm not saying that this journey has been easy. It's taken many years even to get close to the point of feeling comfortable, and along the way there is a lot of insecurity, doubt, shame, and pain.

From the time we are little girls we are taught that we have value. And we are taught that our value is our body—how pretty we are, and how thin we are. It is seared into us that our looks are our contribution to society and to men. We are told that the best thing we can be is desirable to men, and what men desire is pretty and *thin*. That is the *best* thing you can be. You can be smart, funny, successful, a wonderful member of society, and charming, but if you are *overweight* . . . *that* is how you are described. No matter what, if you are thin or have lost weight, you are perceived as looking great and doing fine. It has nothing to do with what is really happening in your life. If you are normal-sized or you have gained weight, people assume your life is shitty.

Not a day goes by where this kind of thinking doesn't seep into my consciousness. It's like a microchip that is embedded in us when we are little and it is almost immovable. But when you are able to have moments of clarity to step back and really look at what's happening in the world, what we should be caring about, how we should be celebrating our lives and living in our excellence and loving one another and our bodies, it is absolutely absurd that our biggest concern is that we are thin. I never grew up being able to throw on tight jeans and a T-shirt and go out into the world, but once I let go of that as the ultimate, I slowly discovered *my* assets, and that is when I found confidence.

Kathy plays an important role in our lives; she represents full-figured women as we are: funny, sexy, smart, and cute. Sure, she's had moments (and months) of doubt. Who hasn't? But it's embracing who she is that gives her the confidence to show the world her "bright lights." Finding out where our secret lies is a journey we're both on. When we discover what it is, we experience ourselves as desirable.

Wickham Boyle is a journalist, financial adviser, and production consultant for theater companies and fashion magazines in New York City. We met through supermodel Emme, and Wickham began to write articles for *Mode.* In love, she has learned to say, "Never say never." Now, second time around, she has a husband she adores, and also two wonderful children.

WICKHAM'S STORY

My first marriage of fifteen years ended. My husband, who verbally degraded me in front of my daughter, left me. To him, I was a "fat pig." I was also recovering from the fact that my ex-husband had tried, but failed, to take the children away from me. Slowly, I began to piece myself and my life back together. I would go to dinner parties, and, to my surprise, three men would give me their cards. I felt like Cher! I thought about what it was that made me attractive. First of all, there's nothing like the solecism of a thirteen-year-old daughter to remind you of what's important in life. I stopped thinking so much about what I looked like. I still have moments. But they are private.

I think that's why my naturally thin daughter is so supportive to women of different sizes. It comes from loving me and from me not exposing her to my insecurities, like "I should be on a diet," or "Do I look fat in this skirt?" Never. I also realized what the marriage had taken away from me. I wanted to be whatever a woman wants: full, whole, intelligent, sexy, vibrant, and smart. No part of a woman should ever be precluded. This is who I am. My beautiful blond socialite friend summed up my attraction. After one of the parties, she said, "We go to a party and every man looks at me, but by the time we leave, every man wants to be with you. I may have the clothes and hair, but you have the personality!" It's my energy and my personality that make me attractive. It's taken a long time to see it, but, by God, I see it now.

Marie St. Victor was born in the Caribbean but moved to upstate New York as a child. In her late thirties, she changed her whole life by going after a dream to become a plus-size model. She walked into my apartment at the beginning of *Mode* (before we had a fashion office) for a casting call, and I saw her beauty reflected through her belief in Spirit. Her inner glow makes her stunning to look at and a pleasure to work with.

MARIE'S STORY

At thirty, I thought the best of me was over. I had thought that men were the only way to validate my attractiveness, until I became spiritually hungry. For the first time in my life, I began a relationship with myself. After reading books on spirituality before breakfast and bed, I realized that I needed to love, respect, and honor myself as a unique and treasured individual. Spending time dining with friends and sitting in Central Park, I started investigating who I was and what I needed in a relationship. I said to myself, Surely my looks can't be the thing that I base my being on. In the past, I had always used my sexuality to validate something that wasn't there. A few laughs with someone didn't make it a relationship. I realized that I had been giving my business away and I'd sold myself cheap. I promised I'd never do that again, because I discovered how valuable I am.

Be open to the experience of being attractive. Give yourself the time to find and celebrate all that makes you attractive to yourself. Use everything we've talked about so far in this book to help you reveal the woman inside: your true self, your self-respect, your flair for style, and the way you make an entrance. And always, but always, be prepared and open to opportunity. You never know when it will knock at your door.

MY STORY

I attended a girlfriend's wedding in Philadelphia some years ago. It was like the movie *My Best Friend's Wedding.* A bearish, handsome Italian-looking man attended. We met over cocktails. We were introduced to each other amid a circle of people. The rest of the group had nothing much to say except "Lovely dress" and "What's the color you use in your hair?" Pleasantries wore thin. Soon, we all found ourselves either looking up at the ceiling or over at the bar. He began smiling at me. Wide and sincere. I could have read it as a polite gesture, but because I was open to the possibility, I knew that it was an admiring glance.

We sipped and exchanged smiles from above our champagne flutes. The group struggled for conversation (we'd discussed everyone's outfit and the color of our hair) and the silences grew longer and more embarrassing. The circle of strangers left two by two to bore another group. We stayed, he and I. And we talked. The conversation was about nothing in particular: We laughed at the bride's brother, now a little tipsy, and discussed what we did, whether we knew the bride or the groom. That sort of thing. The seating plan had put us on opposite corners of the room. By the time dessert was served, I was at his table. Next to him. I asked him to dance, and it felt like the angels sang as the band played into the night.

I ask you to tune in to feeling desirable.

➤ TUNE IN

Think about what you want to feel with someone you love. If you're already in a relationship, think about what makes the relationship special.

Answer these questions in your Learning Curves journal.

1. What makes you special in a relationship?

2. What special qualities would you bring to a relationship, if you're not in one currently?

3. What do you feel you need from a relationship to fulfill you?

4. Do you have that in the relationship you are in?

Now that you've thought about what makes you uniquely lovable, I'd like you to write a love letter to yourself.

1. Write it on beautiful stationery.

2. Describe how a lover feels about you, why he's in love with you, and what the relationship teaches you about yourself and each other.

3. Seal it away in your drawer.

4. When you feel depressed or lost, reread the letter.

5. Remind yourself why you are truly worthy of being loved.

➤ LIVE OUT LOUD

Now that you have a clear description of how you feel about yourself, where do you put it? Answer: out into the world.

Place an ad either on the Internet or in a newspaper or a magazine. Choose carefully. Target the group you want to attract. Read other ads. Educate yourself. Decipher the codes. Here's some help from Lynn Harris, cocreator of the well-known relationship Web site BreakupGirl.com, to help you with writing yours and reading the responses.

1. Don't use unnaturally fanciful euphemisms for the word *fat.* Exceptions: The use of a word derived from a foreign language (*zaftig*) or a fine-arts reference (*Rubenesque*) can do double duty as philistine screeners. Seriously, use a term that you are comfortable with in real life, whether *curvy,* or *big and beautiful,* or just plain *fat.* There's no way to predict what the reader's reaction will be, so you might as well start with what you feel fits. I generally say you should mention size in the first place. People are conditioned to like being surprised even less than they are conditioned to like nonconventional beauty.

2. Do not respond to any ad that refers to a potential mate as "lady."

3. "Seinfeld type" = has weird, annoying friends.

4. "Family-oriented" = mother will attend date.

5. "Fit" = looking for someone who can fit through a door when it's closed.

6. "Takes long walks" = no car.

7. "Sense of humor" = not good enough. A mere "sense" will not fly. Your date must have an actual "grasp" of humor, which is usually evidenced not by declaration, but by an ad that is in itself witty.

8. Keep in mind that your first actual date with a personals person will be exactly like the ad. That is, composed of sentence fragments, half-truths, and morsels (comestible or otherwise) embellished to mask blandness. See? You know exactly what to expect. You'll be just fine.

Remember, you have complete control. You don't have to answer or meet. Go as slowly as you want to. Follow your instincts. And, last word: Any mention of the word *sensual* in his ad usually means he's married and that this is his first affair with a full-figured woman.

FLIRTING SENDS THE FIRST SIGNAL

Are you a flirt? Can you flirt? The man I most recently dated told me that I was an "instinctive flirt." It was a surprise to me. When he declared this, I was so annoyed. How dare he? Flirting was something I watched the other girls do. You know the ones. I really didn't know whether to be pleased or insulted. But he meant it as a compliment. He didn't mean that I was a tease. There's a big difference between openly flirting with genuine admiration and interest and teasing with no actual intention. Don't be afraid to flirt. Express your charm. Flirt in a way that works for you.

KATHY'S STORY

I feel that secretly there are a lot of men and women who are attracted to people who are not thin people. But because of societal pressure, they sometimes choose someone who's more "acceptable." I feel like there's a secret underground attraction and that people don't let themselves act on it. Wherever I see it and identify it, I bring it out. This is because we are taught to be thin and guys are taught they have to have a thin wife or girlfriend. That may not be what they're attracted to. I like to talk about that. That's how I flirt. I get guys to reveal their "secret." On the set of *Veronica's Closet,* all we ever talk about is sex. I think people sometimes find it sexy that I'm open to talking about it. It's fun to flirt and it's fun to see people acknowledge that they may have a different desire than they think they do. Here's another thing that makes you feel confident and want to flirt. At some point, you say, Okay, this is my life. I'm never going to have thin legs and I'll never wear short skirts. Is that the worst fate in life? Let's just jimmy down into my comfort zone and ask myself what good things do I have to work with. It frees me up of so much mind stuff.

Remember, being fuller-figured women does not preclude me or you from flirting. Men can be attracted to our curves, smile, warmth, energy, sense of humor, or our sense of adventure. The way we engage with them is far more seductive than a tight outfit and a heavy lip liner. The trick is to be conscious of the way you behave around people. Do you look people in the eye when you talk to them? I always look men and women in the eye. If you do, you are engaging with someone. That's the first flirt.

WICKHAM'S STORY

My mother would always say to me, "People's eyes are what they were meant to be and their mouth is what they made themselves." Our eyes are what we started with, and so I am not abashed by looking at people's eyes. I love my blue eyes, and not a day goes by where I am not given compliments about them. I found myself in Venice several years ago. I was at a dinner party. I was extremely drawn to the man sitting beside me. I could feel the heat of our chemistry. He spoke broken English and I spoke broken Italian, so we clumsily flirted in both languages. After dinner, when he'd paid the check, he took my hand, led me outside, shoved me against a wall, and kissed me. All the air in Venice was sucked out of the sky. After the kiss, he announced, "I am the host. I must go back inside." We did, and the flirtation continued. I just remember how intense the flirtation became. How I looked had nothing to do with my flirting. I had worn really sexy underwear that night. So I was walking in a way that made me feel really sexy.

Walking and dancing are the most potent signs of seductive body language. When you walk down the street, loosen your hips. Watch the reaction. You'll be amazed how men respond to confidence. They'll feel it. So will you. Men always want to be around the women who look as though they're having the most fun.

MARIE'S STORY

I met a guy named Chris at a party. He seemed like a nice guy. We chatted and flirted until the early hours. When the party had ended, we shared a cab home and realized how many friends we had in common. It became clear that he was also Mr. Helpful. He explained that he could fix anything, so I said that I needed a rod in my closet fixed. By way of thanks, I offered to make him dinner. It was as I got to know him better that I really began to find him attractive. He was a great guy, not just a nice guy. We flirted throughout dinner with our words and innuendos and I found myself opening up to him. He knew how to flirt, and I flirted with the notion that I was the object of his desire.

Ah, yes, words. After the body language and eye contact, words come pretty high up on the flirt list. As we talked about in Step 4, Mind over Matter, how you speak of yourself is a way of telling how good you feel about yourself. If you speak positively about yourself, men will find that attractive about you. Think of how you speak to people in any situation. Do you feel at the top of your game? If you do, men will want to play. Remember, the most flirtatious word we have is *hello.* Use it, and they'll flirt back. But we don't just have to speak in order to flirt. The written word can be as seductive as your voice.

MY STORY

A recent experience of mine showed me how it's what you say, not what you look like, that makes you attractive. As the fashion and style director of *Mode,* I often talk with the reader one-to-one about anything within the realm of fashion and style. In the fall of 1997, I wrote about "sexy stilettos" and "fabulous fishnets," what I had seen on the runways of Paris, New York, and Milan. A European man seemingly fell in love with those words. He'd never met me—just read me. Already, he'd thought I was smart and sexy. A business lunch was arranged with him and his colleague. The three of us met at a downtown eatery. The man greeted me by saying, "I wanted to see if the woman who wrote, 'stilettos are sexy and fishnets are fabulous' was real." I looked at him with a smile and said, "If I had known there had been a request, I may have filled that request." That was the beginning of trouble. The chemistry between us was more explosive than a science project. The female colleague who had joined us for lunch could have dropped under the table and into the earth. We forgot her. Ordering from the menu became a game of flirtation and seduction. The fruitiest wine; oysters as an appetizer; lobster salad to follow; one dessert, two spoons. My mind and body were in overdrive. I thought to myself, Wow, he likes me the way I am. But it was more. He liked me because of who I am. This was true freedom.

Today, I'd like you to tune in to flirting.

➤ **TUNE IN**

In your Learning Curves journal write down the names of all the men you routinely encounter. Choose the ones you are attracted to. If you're in a relationship, write down your partner's name. I'd like you to call him or them "candidates" for your flirting skills. Write about how you act, what you say, how you move, and what you do to flirt.

➤ **LIVE OUT LOUD**

Marilyn Wann—author of the book *Fat!So?* (Berkeley, CA: Ten Speed Press, 1998) and editor of the 'zine of the same title—shares her Flirting 101 workshop exercise. Ask yourself these questions and then go *do* at least one of them each time you are out this month with the men on your list and also strangers. (You will see some of my responses just in case you think I wasn't at that workshop!)

1. Think of three reasons why someone would want you to flirt.

   You can start a conversation. Get the attention of someone you find attractive across the room. You can say something nice to someone else and make them feel good.

2. Think of three reasons why flirting works.

   Because it makes me feel good. Gives me an adrenaline rush. It doesn't cost me anything.

3. Think of three reasons why flirting doesn't work.

   The embarrassment factor, being rejected, no chemistry.

4. Think of three things to say when you're flirting with someone.

   "Do you know who you remind me of?" Or "I'm conducting a survey. . . . " And finally . . . nothing. Just lick your ice cream cone.

5. Think of three types of places where flirting generally happens.

At a party, in an elevator, or on-line.

6. Think of three people (famous ones or people you know) who are great flirts.

Marilyn Monroe, Richard Gere, . . . and me!

Marilyn shared some thoughts with me on the subject of flirting: "Be willing to take the first risk. Flirting is a martial art, and like any other martial art, it is learning how to take a fall without getting hurt. The equivalent of taking a fall in flirting is looking foolish, maybe even being rejected. This is not failure; it is just part of the fun. You are always making the world a better place by flirting. Even if you flop, you are not doing anything wrong; you are doing something wonderful, generous, and courageous."

LEARNING CURVE 26

REJECTION IS PART OF THE GAME

When we play the flirting game, we learn that rejection is the tarot card called "Beyond Hell." Rejection is part of life. We've all been rejected sometime or another and we all know how horrible we feel. We take it personally and it rocks the foundations on which our self-esteem has been built. But let me tell you something: Don't think that the thin blonde with the perfect hairdo who turns heads when she walks into a room hasn't been rejected, either. Ask her.

Many of us immediately jump to the conclusion that men reject us just because of our size. We concoct a fantasy in our heads in which we cast ourselves as the tragic heroine. "How could he?" we say to ourselves, our parents, and our friends. But ask yourself this question: How could he not? As the following stories illustrate, the reason behind why a man has rejected you often has nothing to do with you or your size. It's sometimes as simple as the difference between being a boy or being a girl.

KATHY'S STORY

In a way, I am grateful for growing up as a non-thin child because it meant that I had to come up with other tools to survive. I started observing the people around me, especially the ways boys and girls interacted. I think *that* was the beginning of my feelings of feminism. I realized early on that there were rules. The ways boys could act and the ways girls were supposed to act were completely unbalanced and unfair. Of course, at the time I didn't know it was the seeds of feminism . . . but I kept feeling like: "How come when my friend and I are playing and a boy comes in the room, she becomes a completely different person, stops paying attention to me, and starts flipping her hair and looking down coyly? Why can't we just keep playing? How come it's okay for boys to be adventurous and fun and themselves, but when a boy enters, girls become this 'thing?' " I couldn't do it. I was horrible at changing and didn't get why we had to. As a result I took myself out of the game by gaining weight. It meant I didn't have to be a girlfriend—I could be a girl. Looking back now, I am glad I didn't play the game, but at the time it was so painful.

And then there's the day-to-day stuff of being a non-thin kid: trying to find clothes, going into the "chunky" section of the store with my mom (which was horrifying), being nervous about beach parties, and, of course, not having a boyfriend. I *was* best friends with all the popular football guys, but that was because I was funny, and I hung out with the cutest girls in school. The cute guys hung out with me because I was the one who listened to all of their problems and made them laugh—but I was never, ever the girlfriend.

WICKHAM'S STORY

After my husband left me, I said to myself and my friends, "That's it. I'll never go out with another good-looking man again. I'll never be the less beautiful one in the relationship." But I didn't know what my beauty was. So I began my search. As I undertook the journey to piece myself and my life back together, what I realized more than anything was that if all a man could say in his most angry moments was that I was a "fat pig," then he had no imagination and I actually hadn't done too badly. Rejection is hard, but the loss of myself as a woman was far worse than the words he screamed.

MARIE'S STORY

I was waiting for somebody to make my life right. Make me whole. It was at college that I met an older, sophisticated Australian man. I was fascinated by his mind, humor, and talent. We were together for two years and I thought we had a happy relationship. As we approached our second anniversary, he announced that he was returning to Australia.

I made up my mind to leave my family and friends and go there with him. We went out for a really great dinner, and two days later I ran into him in Central Park. He said that he had meant to call me to let me know that he was leaving for Australia—alone. He had no intention of asking me to go with him. I wanted something that he wasn't willing to give me: himself.

I remember taking a cab home and I wept the whole ride back. The rejection was so painful. I could have held out for a couple of crumbs, but what I really wanted was the sandwich. What I realized was that I had settled for the crumbs. I thought that it couldn't be right that I was with someone and it hurt me so much. What I realize now is that the rejection experience was an opportunity for me to make myself stronger and begin having a relationship with myself before giving my heart away to a man.

MY STORY

My first sexual experience happened when I fell in love with a boy in summer stock. Michael could have had any girl he wanted. (Why do we always say that about physically attractive men?) I was in my early twenties, and this guy was hotter than a jalapeño pepper. I had already started an internal dialogue: He won't find me attractive. What can he possibly see in me? We were never cast opposite each other, but I'd watched him in rehearsals, listened to him deliver his lines, and swooned over him with words of adulation, like "You were *sooo* good!"

After rehearsals one evening, we all went out for drinks. Being an instinctive flirt, I found that Michael was flirting back. Me with all my curves and him with all his angles. A perfect fit? I was willing to find out.

We ended up at my apartment—talking, touching. As much as I was thrilled by the experience, I couldn't help but think, God, what about the lights? The narrow single mattress in my bedroom? The episode of *M*A*S*H* blaring from the TV? But, none of it mattered. I gave myself to him, physically and emotionally. That summer, I'd forgotten my Jewish philosophy on life: marrying a doctor, lawyer, or Indian chief, getting the suburban home and the latest dishwasher. I wanted him. And I had him— for one night. Little did I know that my first sexual experience would be a one-night stand. After that night, he wanted me no more. He was even too embarrassed to look at me. I was completely crushed. Still in pain, though less so by the summer's end, I wrote him a note: "Thank you for making my first sexual experience truly wonderful, even if it was only for one night." Was I crazy? Was I still yearning for him? No, I don't think so. I was just hoping for an answer: Why only one night?

Several weeks later, an engagement announcement arrived. Unexpectedly, it was from Michael. With it came a note. He explained that he had had a great time with me but that he was already involved with a girl from home. That's what had prevented him from seeing me again. I had spent the whole summer torturing myself, thinking that it was all my fault.

I now ask you to tune in to rejection.

➤ TUNE IN

I'd like you to think about the last time you felt rejected. Recall the situation in your mind, the words exchanged, the final scene. Who was he? How did it end? How did you feel? What explanation did he give as to why the relationship was ending? Truthfully, what was he like? Write these questions in your journal and meditate on them. Now I want you to realize the truth of your rejection.

ask yourself:

1. Is it possible he wasn't interested because he's already committed to someone else?

2. Is it possible he wasn't interested because he wasn't ready to commit?

3. It is possible that he wasn't interested because he feared that I'd reject him first?

4. Is it possible that his disinterest really has nothing to do with me, or was he just reacting to my fears?

5. Is it possible that today I am still worthy and okay?

➤ LIVE OUT LOUD

The next time you're rejected, do one or two of the following things, which will make you feel as good about yourself as possible in a difficult situation.

1. Go out with friends to a new club.

2. Plan a weekend vacation with your best friend.

3. Choose one activity from the TLC list that you made in Step 3.

4. Write the letter you want to send to the person to express your hurt, but don't send it. Seal it and burn it. (This one worked for me!)

Marilyn Wann says, "Rejection doesn't last forever. You simply cannot sting from any one rejection for the rest of your life. Even while it hurts, be patient and realize that you'll get over it. You are still fabulous even when you're miserable; you just may not be aware of that. It doesn't make the downs any easier, but there will always be more ups."

Now that you've gotten beyond rejection, it's time for a date.

LEARNING CURVE 27

EVERY RELATIONSHIP BEGINS WITH A DATE

Mention the word *date,* and you probably think you'd rather stay at home and rent a movie. But dating doesn't have to be about feeling clumsy, awkward, or scared. I don't discount the fact that it's often been our experience. All the insecurities resurface: What if he doesn't like me? What if I don't like him? What an ordeal! But think about what dating is.

Dating is about sharing, getting to know someone, and testing the waters. We sometimes feel pressured by the outcome. But I ask you to live in the moment. Don't pressure yourself. Make it an experience you enjoy. If he's not right for you, there's a sea of men waiting for you to dip your big toe into. Take a chance and allow yourself to be open to seeing the bright lights in another.

KATHY'S STORY

Do you remember me going to see the *Stomp* production? Well, I loved it so much that I started to get to know the group, hanging out with them and throwing parties at my house. I hadn't really noticed Dan, one of the actors. During the first party I had at my house, at around three o'clock in the morning, Dan approached me and said, "We're leaving at six to go jump out of an airplane. Do you want to come?" I said, "Okay." Everyone began piling into different cars, and Dan got into the front seat of my Mustang convertible. I thought to myself, Okay, whatever, I'll talk to this young guy. I was so not caring. I was wearing sweatpants, my hair was pulled back in a loose knot, and I had no idea that he would be anybody that I would be attracted to. As we drove, he became funnier and funnier, smarter and smarter. By the end of the two-hour drive, he emerged as a face and a person. He was so attractive to me. We had to jump out of the airplane in twos. We chose to jump together. That was our first date, our first meeting. It wasn't awkward; it was amazing.

Dates do not have to be formally arranged. They can happen anywhere: Airplanes, vacations, personal ads, and even on-line are great ways to meet people and get to know someone. It doesn't matter what you wear. You just have to show up as yourself. Restaurant dates can be intimidating, especially if the menu is written only in French. But if you are open to the experience of dating, you are open to something quite beautiful.

WICKHAM'S STORY

My "no good-looking men" rule was about to be blown out of the water. Although I was back on the dating scene, no one had felt right. If I went on a bad date, I'd call Heather, my twenty-two-year-old baby-sitter, from the rest room of a restaurant and ask her to call the maître d'. He'd tell me there was an emergency at home and I had to leave right away. I had seen Zachary at a party. I had met him twenty years ago and saw him at various parties throughout that time. He had tried to get me to go out with him on a date for three months. I said to myself that I wasn't going out with him because I was over good-looking men!

I had been feeling pretty low and I hadn't been answering the phone. Heather was with me one night after the children had gone to bed. We had rented our favorite movies and were fast-forwarding to the make-out scenes. Watching the part in *The Big Easy* where Dennis Quaid kisses Ellen Barkin, I turned to Heather and said, "Do you think anyone will kiss me like that again?" At that moment, the phone rang. Heather answered and heard a voice that made Barry White's sound unmellifluous. Heather put the receiver down and said, "You have to talk to this guy; he's got the most amazing voice." Well, I had to look cool in front of a twenty-two-year-old! It was Zachary. He said that he had to meet me. Two nights later, he showed up with four dozen red tulips. I couldn't believe it.

Let me tell you about Zachary. He's tall, smooth-talking, and extraordinarily handsome. He took my hand and I felt myself sink into his buttery grip. We went to a restaurant, and I was wearing nothing wonderful: Levi's rolled up, sandals, a white man's shirt over a black lace bra, my father's black Yves Saint Laurent jacket, Annick Goutal perfume, pearl earrings and necklace. But I felt great. I can smell the perfume to this day when I think of the date. Dinner was fabulous, and it wasn't just the food. We laughed from beginning to end. As he escorted me home, I gave him a peck on the cheek. Disappointed, he asked me if I would give him a real kiss. Of course I would! And I did.

Wicki could have missed the opportunity of spending a wonderful evening with an attractive man if she had left her heart and mind closed. A friend told her that she can be out of the house for twenty minutes and a lifetime will have passed in front of her. Opportunities present themselves daily. But how open are you to creating that opportunity? We must never try to stand in our own way—even when the going gets a little rough.

MARIE'S STORY

Whenever I prepared for a date, I tried to look as relaxed as possible. Little did they know. Date dressing was a ritual. I used to put on party music, pour myself a glass of wine, lay out the makeup, and start to paint. I'd try on a few different clothes, since I felt that I was getting ready for war. My hair took forever to style. I spritzed Emanuel Ungaro's Diva perfume. Finally, two hours later, I was out the door.

My dates with Chris were much less of a production. What I loved to wear on our dates were sweaters, jeans, and cowboy boots. We'd go to each other's houses, have dinner, and cuddle up on the sofa, listening to Ella Fitzgerald, Louis Armstrong, forties jazz. I had become extremely attracted to him. We had made out several times, and he brushed it off as being "just good friends." What did he mean, "just good friends"? He was pushing himself away from me at the same time as feeling attracted to me.

We drove to meet his parents and the radio was playing Randy Travis. The lyrics were, "I know you want to break up and leave." I thought that's how he felt. But he was the one feeling scared that I'd break up with him. I could feel my heart icing up once more. I prayed to God, thinking, If this is the man you want me to be with, melt my heart.

The next day, it melted. I was at work and a letter came through the fax machine for me. It was a love letter from Chris, the likes of which I have never read or received before. He actually started to talk. Really talk. We spoke our truths. It was only then that we were ready to take the first steps to building a relationship with each other.

MY STORY

I can remember a date when I was feeling great and raring to go. Of course, that doesn't mean I wasn't nervous. I discovered how to turn a potentially awkward situation around. Remember "personal ad Bobby"? Well, we decided to go on our first date. On the night we had arranged for Bobby to pick me up to take me to dinner, I came home from work, showered, and dressed in my long-sleeved black dress. I felt seductive. I looked in the mirror, reapplied a red lip, gave a last look, and smiled. At 7:30 P.M., the doorbell rang. Remember, he was a man from a personal ad. I had never seen him. I opened the door, and a short, mustached man with sandy brown hair who was clutching a bouquet of flowers greeted me. It didn't matter how he looked. We had spoken several times on the phone, and already I was attracted to him. So there we were, two strangers—bar the phone conversations—face-to-face over a perfectly laid table. My mind was thinking a million things at once. What does he think of me? What do I think of him? What will I order? Do I eat the bread? Do I eat dessert? What if I go overboard and eat too much?

I realized how crazy I had become. So I politely excused myself and headed for the rest room. On the way, I reminded myself that he was probably nervous, too. I looked in the mirror, took a deep breath, and whispered some of my positive affirmations to help calm me down. With composure and a smile, I returned. I finally relaxed and, yes, we had the best time. My hands and lips were painted Chanel red and he was visibly fascinated by them. So my gestures became more exaggerated. I put my hands on my cheek and through my hair, then on his hands. Back at home, Bobby's sweet and simple good-night kiss on my living room sofa sealed the end of a perfect evening.

Now, tune in.

➤ TUNE IN

In your Learning Curves Journal, write down the experience of your perfect date. What are you wearing? How do you look and feel? Where are you? Whom are you with? Make it real.

➤ LIVE OUT LOUD

Here are some tips that will help you date with style and confidence.

PREPARING FOR THE DATE

I believe that it's important to prepare for dating as much as for the date itself. Even if you don't have one on the horizon, being prepared will support your belief that a date's in your future. So, always act as if you're dating. I do, even when I'm not. You can, too, by following this dating checklist.

1. OUTFIT

Have date clothes especially reserved for when the occasion arises. It prevents the sudden and desperate need to rush out and buy something that you vow to return the following Monday, only to have had a glass of red wine spill on the jacket during the date.

Wear your favorite silhouette and color.

Remember to dress your assets. I'm sure you now know what they are. Refer to the list on page 144 to help you choose how to dress to show your strengths. And remember, it's all in the details: Think about fabrics. Luxurious fabrics, like silk, satins, velvet, and cashmere, will help you feel special. What fabrics do you want to touch and be touched by?

2. LINGERIE

Your white cotton panties may be fine for everyday, but you want to feel sexy. Try a demicut push-up bra, a lace panty set, or a bodysuit. Even if he never knows, it'll make *you* feel great.

3. ACCESSORIES

Shoes affect the way you walk and feel. If your shoes aren't new, ensure that they're buffed or polished. If you opt for open-toed shoes, I have three words to say on the subject: Pedicure! Pedicure! Pedicure! And that reminds me: Always look after your hands—they speak a thousand languages, and are an extension of your femininity. Remember, many men are fascinated by manicured fingers.

Think sexy.

As for jewelry, let your taste rule. But remember, simpler pieces will keep the focus more on you.

4. TEST RUN

Try on the whole look and check yourself out in the mirror. How do you feel? Sexy, beautiful, and alluring, I hope. This is how you want your clothes to feel. If not, don't worry, you can always make another choice. This is why I always recommend the test run.

When it comes to the day of your date, you'll feel confident to know that you're already prepared in the wardrobe department. This will take the stress away from how you look, so you can spend your energy on how you feel. It's important to feel centered, confident, and beautiful if you are to relax and enjoy yourself.

5. TAKE TIME GETTING READY

Remember your TLC list. I always luxuriate in a warm bath, scented with oils, and the bathroom is lit with candles and incense. This will help you feel unhurried and help to soothe any feelings of anxiety you may have.

6. CHECK IN WITH YOURSELF

When you're dressed and ready, stand in front of the mirror and say a few of your favorite affirmations, then walk out the door and have a fabulous time. Allow yourself to shine. Feel your best and enjoy the date.

LEARNING CURVE 28

RELATIONSHIPS ARE BUILT ONE BRICK AT A TIME

When the dating gets serious, the next step is often the mutual commitment to building a relationship, a life together. It's a step that signifies not only a commitment to friendship and love but also a vow, ceremonial or otherwise, to share your life's joint learning curves. Follow them and see where they lead you.

Dr. Nicki Berke, a relationship expert, says, "We've all heard the expression 'Beauty is as beauty does.' Nice, but slightly wrong—actually, 'Beauty is as beauty feels.' If you want to build a healthy relationship with someone else, start by building a relationship with yourself. Appreciate your feelings, identify your thoughts, understand your actions, and change your behavior. Build your relationship one brick at a time from the inside out."

KATHY'S STORY

The reason I fell in love with Dan was that I had never met anyone who loved women as much as he did. He really loved his mom and his friends who were girls. That made me, as the girlfriend, feel really comfortable. Especially sexually. He made me feel so secure, even with my thirty years of body issues. He was very positive, praising, encouraging, and appreciative. It didn't even seem like he was trying hard to make me feel safe. Let me tell you, within six weeks, all of my hang-ups were gone. I had no more issues. That's the kind of woman I think everyone wants sexually.

While Dan toured the country with *Stomp,* I went with him to all the cities. It was a nine-month tour and so much fun for me. We had made a commitment to each other that we'd start a life together in California when he finished touring. Dan, thirteen years my junior, and I moved in together and we had a baby girl we cherish. Two years later, on August 8, 1998, we married. I'm so happy that we found each other. No—that we *chose* each other.

WICKHAM'S STORY

After the dinner date, and many more wonderful moments, Zachary and I got married a year and a half later. We never know all the things that draw other people to us. But I love Zachary and I know he loves me. He always says that he loves my ass and my legs; two of the things I'm most sensitive about. Zachary tells me all the time how much he adores me and that I should just be comfortable and love myself. I'm on that journey.

But I'll tell you why I love him. Last summer in Italy with the children, we drove a car to Rome. We were just chatting, as you do on vacation. The question we asked one another was, "If you could make one wish, what would it be?" My fair-skinned daughter wished that she had tanned skin. We all came up with wishes. Zachary just said, "I wish that everyone was comfortable with who they are, and then no one would have any wishes." This man was sent to me. For fifteen years, I had the meanest man God could have sent me, because I wasn't ready for anything else. I didn't stand up and say, "This is the *wrong* size. I'm taking it back!" After Zachary and I married, I used to roll over in bed and think, I don't believe this. But what kind of message did that send out into the universe? I *can* believe it. I have exactly what I deserve: the best.

MARIE'S STORY

At forty-one years old, I got married. It was to Chris, and my wedding was magical. I remember grown men crying as we took our vows. I could not believe that I ever thought that after thirty, the best of me was over. It took me a while to discover what the best of me meant. I realize that I need affection, attention, connection, mutual respect, and friendship. That's what I have. A couple of weeks ago, I asked Chris why he loved me. He said, "I love you because I appreciate your strength, that you love God, and for the way you take care of people." Chris and I had tried for a child a year ago and I lost the baby. Every Mother's Day, he gives me flowers. I sometimes find it overwhelming that I am loved so much. I am so grateful for all the joy and grace in my life. What I realize is that everything starts with the feelings I have about myself. I love myself and I see the ripple effect it has on my husband, friends, family, and the spiritual congregation I adore.

I have yet to meet my soul mate, but it doesn't stop me from enjoying and sharing myself with a man. Armed with a confidence of knowing who I am, I have learned how to date with style.

MY STORY

If you ask me what I have been waiting for, it would be the right moment and the feeling of complete abandon to let loose. I arrived in the beautiful seaport town of Naples (what's *in* the Italian air?) on a sunny day in March, after the Bologna Fall Fashion Shoe Fair, to tour the factories and see how the famous Italian shoes are made. Sitting in the office of the president of one of the largest factories, I saw Massimo again. Already the feeling of liquid attraction entered my body. He smiled and we talked. Dinner was arranged by my host, and I found myself in a puddle of possibility. I decided to slick my hair back and throw on a slinky, sexy jersey outfit with a high slit up the back of my skirt. Then I walked down to the concierge's desk. He confirmed what I already knew. I looked and felt *bellissima*. Of course, only Italy would celebrate women with a yearly spring holiday, Women's Day. The Italians showered us all day with lovely yellow mimosa flowers. I could not believe I was in Naples, in Italy, where men love women. Each curve, smile, sigh, and movement is celebrated in all the streets, doorways, and rooms across this verdant country.

Off to dinner, and Massimo and I were placed side by side. The smile began and I smiled seductively. Every tilt of my head or movement of my hand made him watch—watch *me*. Wine was poured into the waiting goblets. The oysters came, and I slid them down my throat with glee as he watched. The pasta came, and I slowly slurped the noodles down, catching his eyes. The shrimp had to be taken out of their shells. Undressing my main course was a silent striptease. And then the dessert—yes, especially the dessert—captivated my fan club of one. The frozen gelato was presented in whole walnut shells and the skins of passion fruit. Each bite, chew, and swallow was a message. He responded by saying, "You must stop." More sweets came to the table. The Italian word *baci* means "kiss," and of course Baci chocolate has a love message wrapped inside its foil paper. Where else but in Italy? The dessert wine, Frambolino, drink of the goddesses, was brought to the table. It comes from the small, delicate strawberries grown wild in the woods. The feeling of pure nectar ran through the wine in the glasses, and my entire body. A hand placed on the small of my back confirmed the moment. Who knew that food could be such a sensual experience?

Dinner ended and we walked toward the castle. We found ourselves sitting on the benches near the docking area of the port, where the boats come in at night. We listened to the waves lap up against the sailboats. As we began to walk, he turned to me and said, "This is the perfect place to kiss a beautiful woman." I was lost. A feeling of calm and excitement raced through me at the same time. The taste still reels in my mouth. It is said that Italy is the most sensual place to experience life to the fullest: Food, love, and the cities themselves are a visual feast. I agree, and will savor each memory with a smile. It's moments like these that have allowed me to be open to having a relationship as passionate as the color of the Italian sunsets.

Feel the power you have as a woman.

➤ **TUNE IN**

Now that you're beginning to see that you—yes, you—can have and deserve a wonderful relationship, I want you to continue to ensure that you are really being open to receiving it. Answer these questions in your journal:

1. Am I still living in fear of past relationship experiences and rejections?
2. Am I consciously working to acknowledge and remember why I am worthy and desirable?

➤ **LIVE OUT LOUD**

If you answered yes to the first question, you need to reread Step 1 and use the techniques we discussed that will allow you to release past experiences. If you answered no to the second question, you need to create and use affirmations that acknowledge your beauty and worth.

So, wherever you are on your learning curve, I ask you today to make a promise. Never settle for anything less than what you deserve. Feel the power you have as a woman. And yes, there is more of you to love. Live in today and share the best of who you are. That, my friend, is all of you.

Step 8

Being a Role Model with Style

I think all women can be role models for one another. In fact, we already are, whether we like it or not. We look at one another's lives and compare them to our own. Although we don't like to admit we do this, we do. Be true to yourself and not to what others think you should be.

EMME, SUPERMODEL, AUTHOR, AND SPOKESPERSON

REALIZE THAT YOU MAKE A DIFFERENCE

The eighth step on the learning curve recognizes the role model in each of us. Yes, you and I, every woman in this book, and anyone whose life you've touched or changed. We are all role models. To our children, family, friends, and the strangers on the street at whom we smile. We affect each other's lives in many ways, often so subtle that we aren't always aware we're making a difference. We are.

Celebrities are our most visible role models. Their every sound bite, project, and unique style is recorded for the world to read and watch. Their familiarity draws admiration, even adoration and trust. Sharing their insights and experiences helps us to make new choices and to see new paths. If they can do it, we can. They empower us with the capacity to believe that anything is possible as long as we hold the vision that we are who we are. Our role models offer us hope, comfort, and support.

In your life, you have every opportunity to become a role model to others. Our efforts are just as significant, endearingly human, equally touching, and similarly profound as those of our role models. Sometimes our role models are right in front of us. One of whom is my mother's dearest friend, Roz Spencer. She has such a full life, dresses with great style, breaks every rule by having many of her clothes custom-made, and she *owns* her body. But the most amazing quality about her is that she has taught her daughters to be proud of who they are no matter what their size. To me, she is an example of someone who has always lived her life in full and with style. Roz is a true role model.

If you can make a positive difference in just one person's life, you'll see how special and gifted you are. The women in this chapter, some of the friends you've come to know in this book, recognize the role model in themselves. Each is proud of what she represents: for women, to women, and as a woman.

KIM COLES

Why shouldn't I be the best of me as often as possible? Especially when it comes to being a role model to young women. I had amazing female role models. In particular, my aunts and my mother. All were strong, stylish, beautiful, funny women, with minds of their own, careers they loved, and a sense of warmth and love of the world around them. I looked in the mirror recently and saw all of them staring back at me. I've become the woman I've wanted to be. Just like them. I do have a friend whom I watched go through an amazing transformation due to the love and patience I gave him. He was a manic-depressive, pill-popping alcohol abuser. In short, a *mess.* But he was also a brilliant human being who was not living anywhere near up to his potential. He went through hell and back and took me with him for the ride! However, through a long process and an intervention on my part, he gained the strength to figure himself out and find a positive path. He thanks me for my friendship, patience, unselfishness, and for believing in him. I'm glad I was there to help in any way I could.

KATE DILLON

As a professional model, I hope to make things easier for other women, especially younger women, with regard to body image. The public speaking I engage in has been the most profound journey for me. During Eating Disorders Awareness Week, Harvard University asked me if I would like to share my story with other women. I agreed. I spoke on a stage in front of 350 women. My speech comprised all my life experiences. After I spoke, I spent forty-five minutes answering questions for an enthusiastic audience. During the same week, I was asked to speak to a group of Girl Scouts. They were all between the ages of eight and eleven. They listened intently. When I finished, one of the girls stood up and said to me, "I'm the leader of the women's group at school and we have pictures of you all over our wall." I just thought, Wow! I was so impressed by them. Even at their age, they were so aware and embracing of themselves. Each of them really wanted to hear what I had to say. In some way, I think it was a relief for them to hear my message. They were like, "Oh, you mean we don't have to walk around feeling bad about ourselves? That's really cool." At the end of that week, sharing my story and opening girls and women to a new idea, I realized one thing: how right I am, how right Michele is, how right we all are in thinking that something can change. Thinking that we can create awareness and a change of social conscious- ness. It's so important both to embrace individuality and celebrate the dif- ferences we have among ourselves.

EMME

I have a need to be true to myself and not be what others think I should be. I think this is an important message to pass on to our youth. I believe I affect others through my stick-to-itiveness, and by not aban- doning my belief that women are able to and must use their own voices in this most incredible democratic society. I knew I had to continue speaking to young men and women about finding a healthy body image and positive self-esteem after I met a young Hispanic twelve-year-old girl at a local junior high school. It was following one of my first lectures in 1994, just after I was featured in *People* magazine's 50 Most Beautiful People issue. In the com- motion after the lecture, a girl patiently waited until everyone got auto- graphs and asked their questions before she approached me. She told me that I was the reason she hadn't taken her life the weekend before. She explained that her mother was relentless about her early-developed body and that her mother thought she was being very promiscuous. Obviously, there were mixed messages coming from her mom, and that was confusing to her young daughter. What was really happening was that the mother's boyfriend was hitting on the girl and the mother found out. The mother began to blame the girl for *his* indiscretions. Unreal, but true. Despite the fact that she was crying out for help, this young woman was not being heard, and her self-esteem and body image were being trashed for no reason other than her mother's lack of judgment. As I saw how her body was being blamed for the boyfriend's indiscretions, I realized how many people value themselves only through their bodies. I felt the need to address the issue with other adolescents. I wanted to help young people see beyond their bodies in order to value themselves as creative, special, and unique individuals who have incredible things to offer the society they live in. My life was never the same after that encounter.

DEE DEE KNOCHE

It's so important for me to be true to myself. I try to make a difference daily, be it baby-sitting so that parents can spend some time with each other, or just by being kind. I love baby-sitting. I look after three girls, all nine years old, and they inspire me as much, if not more, than I do them. There's something so magical about children. They are both curious and think they know it all, they say things without editing themselves, and they speak the truth. I get so much out of baby-sitting, and it feels good to know that I'm helping people out.

What I also do to help others is to donate time. Like Michele, I carve out some time to aid the Dress for Success organization. Donating my time makes each woman feel special. I was doing makeup for one woman who had been incarcerated. As I got to know her better, I just looked at her and realized that she was no different from the women on Madison Avenue. It was just that she was given different life circumstances. We should all work on appreciating diversity. The only way to survive is to be kind to people.

CAMRYN MANHEIM

I'm really proud of what I've accomplished in the face of great adversity. I feel very powerful and am very conscious of how I present myself in public, in front of the cameras, and at awards ceremonies. Fashion may not seem important to most people, but for a group of women in particular who have been excluded in this arena, something as simple as fashion becomes a huge political statement. There was a time when I couldn't have given a shit about fashion because fashion didn't care about me. That's all changed. Fortunately, designers have now stepped on the plus-size bandwagon. Many designers knew the press would be paying attention to me at awards ceremonies like the Emmys. Many of them called and asked if they could design my gown. But when I asked these designers if they made plus-size clothes most of them said no, so I felt I had a responsibility to full-figured girls to make sure that I was wearing something that they could purchase as well. Not just a one-time-only Armani gown. That was one simple way that I could include women who have fought the same battles I have.

I realize that because I am in the public eye, people are listening to what I say and watching what I do, and I take that responsibility very seriously. All my life I was looking for a positive role model whom I could look up to. Now that I'm in a position to be to be that for others, I want to make sure that I am always imparting an empowering message. When I'm asked to attend a benefit or participate in a charity event, I don't just show up and smile for the cameras without knowing exactly what the organization is trying to achieve. Since I know my voice is so loud now, I use my platform wisely.

VANESSA MARSHALL

From confusion and self-loathing to serenity and self-acceptance, my journey has taken me down some interesting avenues. Through learning to be myself, I believe I have had the largest impact on women around me. When I graduated from Princeton with honors, I was pretty psyched. But greater than this accomplishment was being asked to be the godmother to my English professor's daughter. My professor claimed to have witnessed a great commitment on my part in women's studies and the arts, to seeking my truth and to honoring myself with integrity and intention. She respected me. She applauded the creative risks I took at Princeton. My senior thesis, directing Gertrude Stein's play *Photograph,* dealt with self-image and the language used to describe the self. The show dared the female viewers to question the patriarchal constructs and customs so easily accepted as "normal." I tried to awaken the viewers, and my professor celebrated that.

You see, what I found is that my creativity is now supported by love, not fear. When people witness my creative acts in my one-woman show and through my stand-up comedy, they ask how I can take such risks. I believe that my path is to let other women see how they have accepted themselves. That is the key. When I communicate this, I believe I encourage self-love in others around me. I dare my friends to do what they fear most, as I do, no matter what size they are. I say, "This is not a dress rehearsal until you are a size whatever. Do it now!" As a result, I have watched my girl-friends step into their power despite their fears. My philosophy, my style, is that the time is now. I live by that and I think the benefits of this worldview encourage women around me to do the same. We should all dare to love ourselves and follow that path toward the kind of abundance we are all enti-tled to enjoy. Today, I am indeed a godmother. I am grateful to stand up and carry the torch to help her find her bliss, her truth, and her inner beauty. When I stand up onstage, it is such an affirmation of my internal shift toward celebrating myself. All of me. Every time I begin a stand-up routine, the sparkle in my eyes is evidence of my journey and my victory.

ANGELLIKA MORTON

I realize that I can do everything regardless of size. I have found my gift, my style. We all have to sit back and think about what we enjoy most in life and then follow that passion. I have had my picture taken for *Mode* and recently I was stopped in Central Park. A young black girl named Renée started running after me. She followed me around the park, saying, "Excuse me?" I turned to her, and she proclaimed, "You're my idol. My therapist has me reading *Mode* because I have an eating disorder." She was thin. Renée continued: "I look at your pictures and I think you're so beautiful." I was shocked and flattered. Shocked that such a young, thin girl was already seeing a therapist and flattered that she took the time to tell me that I was her idol. If I can help one young girl with her body image and eating disor-der, no matter what her size, I feel that I am playing my part as a role model in someone else's life. That's who I am. I felt so proud that Renée told me that I had made a difference to her.

KATHY NAJIMY

I think it would be faux modest of me to say that I don't think I'm a role model. All the letters I receive tell me I am. I know I am. I've been very blessed to have been given recognition for doing certain things. Of course, you start out thinking that no one's going to pay attention to anything you do. Recently, I was talking to my husband after I came home from this meeting about being the spokesperson for a plus-size lingerie line. I thought how funny it was that I had started out as this poor, chubby girl from San Diego who was identified by her size and now I was being asked to stand up and be applauded for encouraging women to wear this beautiful lingerie. How weird is the world that my nonthin size has turned into recognition and praise? It's great. I never could have predicted that my fat would win!

My goal is always to make a decision with integrity. I don't always succeed and I often fall short, but integrity is my goal. It isn't easy. Sometimes, you don't get hired, and you fight, you argue, you're ignored, and you're lied to. There are a million obstacles. But I feel people appreciate my integrity. My character on *Veronica's Closet* is a role model. I don't play a victimy fat girl. I wear beautiful clothes and I have young, beautiful boyfriends, which is reflected in real life. Olive, my character, is very sensual, doesn't complain about her weight, doesn't whine about being single, and, to the producers' credit, the show doesn't degrade plus-size women. I also go on talk shows and speak about issues that I think are important to women. That's being a role model for people, because when you come to Hollywood, you're supposed to lose all of your concerns and just care about plastic surgery. I care about all my issues. I'm an AIDS, gay and lesbian, animal, and women's activist. That's refreshing to people, because I think people expect actresses to be shallow, self-serving, and self-absorbed. Also, I look like more people in everyday American life than the girls on *Friends* do. There are more people who have sisters, wives, girls down the street, teachers, and classmates who look like me than women who weigh eighty pounds. For me, being plus-size makes me a role model, because people say, "Oh yeah, I know her; that's more like what I know."

When I lost weight, I got a lot of offers to do books, videos, and TV appearances about losing weight. I said no. It was because, first of all, who knew how long I was going to keep the weight off? Also, I didn't want more women to have more pressure. Women already feel enough pressure to be a different way. I didn't want to be any kind of inspiration or pressure for women. We need to start living our lives. Live life now. As you know, I do a lot of work with AIDS, and it hit me about five years ago that even though I had fat thighs, at least I had thighs. There are people all around us dying and not able to use their bodies. We should be thankful for our bodies. Let's be grateful. I always smile at full-figured women because their heads are usually down. I tell them they are beautiful. All women are role models. Everybody has a light.

ANNA SCHOLZ

I receive a lot of letters from women who are encouraged by the work I do in helping them to feel better about themselves. It's my mission. One experience particularly moved me. A newspaper magazine in London wrote an article about me. From that feature alone, I received five hundred phone calls and twenty letters. One letter in particular arrived from an anonymous woman. The lady said that it was 5:00 A.M. and she had been feeling depressed. She had gained weight and "friends" of hers had been tormenting her by saying, "How can you let yourself down so much? Why did you become a size eighteen? How can you do this to yourself?" She happened to read the article and wrote that she was so encouraged by what I was doing that she was going to photocopy it and send it to all her "friends." "When I come to London," she said, "I'll buy one of your outfits." She ended the letter by saying that she felt I was so strong and sexy and that we needed to have more pictures like this in the press. That's exactly what I want to provoke in people. I ask women to question the hang-ups they have and accept themselves now, rather than constantly wanting to change. I'm not saying that all women should be big, only that they take care of themselves and not stop themselves from feeling good about themselves today.

MICHELE WESTON

In all the conversations I've had with the extraordinary women in this book, I feel that the thing that makes us role models is that we are as proud of our failures as we are of our successes. What makes us individual and different? Sometimes it's as plain as the nose on our face, the curve of a hip, the shape of our legs.

The women who inspire me and touch my life all have one thing in common. Each of them truly lives in her body and they share themselves honestly with everyone they meet. Many are a very special breed of model—plus-size models. Why are they role models to me? It is because in the face, literally, of being told that they are not the "ideal," they create their own ideal. I can remember going out to style my first fashion story with Kate Dillon and having the photographer turn to me as we began that morning and say, "How do I do this?" I responded, "Find out what is in her that makes her so sexy." As he began to shoot, the photographer turned to me and smiled. He captured what we could all see and feel.

Through my journey, I have learned that each woman is her own ideal, her own best reflection. A couple of years ago, we shot a *Mode* cover with fourteen models—all a size fourteen. We chose women from different backgrounds, of different color, height, and curves, to illustrate that each woman individually possesses her own style and beauty. Talk about a learning curve. When you look at the fashion pages of a magazine, look into the models' eyes. See what's inside them that is being captured on the page.

I have always said that I never wanted to be anybody else but me. I believe that. Without my experiences and learning, I would not be the woman I am today. The last twenty years of my life have taught me a great deal about myself. What makes me a role model is that I feel I don't have to change, fit in, or agree with anyone other than myself. Proudly, I stand in my own shoes. I believe that women have to use their voices. With *Mode*, I have used my voice to help all full-figured women look stylish and celebrate their curves. My bravery to look first at who I am inside and then take the punches, go to bat, and fight our cause has given me the courage to claim my style. If I can affect one mother so that her daughter has a different opportunity to experience her life or teach one woman to change the way she feels about herself, I will have succeeded in making a difference.

You, my friend, are also a role model to the people in your life.

> **TUNE IN**

You may think you don't affect the world, but you do. In your Learning Curves journal:

1. List the five people you most admire who are living.

2. List the five people you most admire who are dead.

3. List five qualities that these people have in common.

4. List five qualities you admire in yourself.

5. List five people who admire you.

> **LIVE OUT LOUD**

Now you can take some actions to do something to help someone. Choose one action from this list. You may find that you like a number of these suggestions, so try them on for size.

1. Join an organization like Meals on Wheels or God's Love We Deliver and help take food to homebound people.

2. If you have a skill like math or reading, offer your skills to groups such as Northern Lights Alternatives, Big Brother or Big Sister programs, or Headstart to help a young person in school.

3. Help a member of your family with an upcoming project for work or college.

4. Donate clothing to an organization that helps women get back on their feet during or after a difficult time, so they can start a new chapter in their lives.

5. Find out if your religious organization needs help with any programs, or lead a seminar for young adults on a subject you're fluent in.

6. Teach a class to your daughter's Girl Scout troop about how language concerning our bodies affects others.

7. Work on an upcoming political race and show that you are part of making a difference in your government.

8. Take a child to the park or zoo and teach her about nature.

9. Explain to your daughter that it is okay to say no when she feels threatened.

10. Walk for the Cure or wear a pink ribbon in October, Breast Cancer Awareness Month.

I'd like you to realize that *you* make a difference. You are a role model as a mother and daughter, teacher and student, friend and lover, adviser and listener. I invite you to be all that you are.

This journey is at an end *and* a beginning. My hope is that you can see the woman you are—unmasked, fully clothed, self-assured. As I've said, what makes us role models is that we stand up, fall down, and proudly stand back up. We have grown with strength. We are original and different and should be truly grateful to be so. For each of us *is* different and special. That is the gift of the role model. It is your gift.

Realize that your style is like your favorite record. Your body may play the bass and your clothes may play the tune, but your style is the final composition—it's the complete song you're singing. Most of all, style gives you your voice. Some of us play a jazzy tune, and some of us hum a melody that's soft and lyrical. We each sing a different song. That's the beauty of individual style. Those who have inspired you in this book and in your lives are all singing. In unison but solo, in harmony but with distinction. Through tears and laughter, joy and pain.

We each have a responsibility to ourselves and those around us. It is to inspire others and aspire to be the best of who we are. Sing your song. You don't have to think long and hard about being a role model. You already are. Look around. Celebrate your manner of being and doing—*your* style. Appreciate the people in your life who stay with you through thick and thin. Treasure those people. Learn from them as they learn from you.

With all that I have shared on how to live your life in full and with style, I hope that you start to see how much you have to offer in, of, and as yourself. Take in all your accomplishments and embrace the struggles. Smile at your children for getting the new job. See the gifts you bring to the table with your own life. Hold the vision that you are a first-rate version of yourself. Without imitation. Without limitation. Just *you.* So today, my friend, ask yourself, "Why shouldn't I be brilliant, gorgeous, talented, and fabulous?" Actually, you already are.

Additional Reading

Burke, Delta, and Alexis Lipsitz. *Delta Style*. New York: St. Martin's Press, 1998.

Coles, Kim. *I'm Free But It'll Cost You*. New York: Hyperion, 1997.

Deckert, Barbara. *Sewing for Plus Sizes*. Connecticut: Taunton Press, 1999.

Emme with Daniel Paisner. *True Beauty*. New York: Perigee Books, 1998.

Erdman, Cheri, ed. *Nothing to Lose*. New York: Harper Collins, 1996.

Fraser, Laura. *Losing It: False Hopes and Fat Profits in the Diet Industry*. New York: Penguin, 1998.

Gaesser, Glenn A., Ph.D. *Big Fat Lies: The Truth About Your Weight and Your Health*. New York: Fawcett Columbine, 1996.

Hirshmann, Jane R., and Carol H. Munter. *When Women Stop Hating Their Bodies*. New York: Fawcett Columbine, 1995.

Hutchinson, Marcia Germaine. *Transforming Body Image*. Trumansburg, NY: Crossing Press, 1995.

LeShan, Lawrence. *How to Meditate*. New York: Bantam, 1984.

Lyons, Pat, and Debby Burgard. *Great Shape*. San Francisco: Bull Publishing, 1990. website: www.bodypositive.com

Manheim, Camryn. *Wake Up, I'm Fat!* New York: Broadway Books, 1999.

Orbach, Susie. *Fat Is a Feminist Issue II*. New York: Berkley Press, 1982.

Poulton, Terry. *No Fat Chicks: How Big Business Profits by Making Women Hate Their Bodies*. New York: Birch Lane Press, 1997.

Sark. *Succulent Wild Women: Dancing with Your Wonder-Full Self*. New York: Fireside, 1997.

Seid, Roberta Pollack. *Never Too Thin: Why Women Are at War with Their Bodies*. New York: Prentice-Hall, 1989.

Tribole, Evelyn, and Elyse Resch. *Intuitive Eating*. New York: St. Martin's Press, 1996.

Wann, Marilyn. *Fat!So? Because You Don't Have to Apologize for Your Size*. Berkeley, CA: Ten Speed Press, 1998. website: www.fatso.com

Wolf, Naomi. *The Beauty Myth*. New York: William Morrow, 1991.

Index

Index